PRODUCERS AND CONSUMERS IN EU E-COMMERCE LAW

Producers and Consumers in EU E-Commerce Law argues that the European Union is failing adequately to protect consumers' critical interests in e-commerce. The book compares the Union's close protection of producers' critical interests in e-commerce, considered in terms of authorship and of 'domain-identity', with its faltering steps towards protection of consumers' corresponding interests, considered in terms of fair trading, privacy and (on behalf of children) morality. The book assesses the threats posed to those interests, the extent to which self-help can and does neutralise those threats and, as regards any gaps left, the extent to which the Union has stepped into the breach. The argument is important given that surveys show low levels of consumer confidence in European cross-border e-commerce, a motor of integration *par excellence*.

Producers and Consumers in EU E-Commerce Law

JOHN DICKIE
University of Leicester

·HART·
PUBLISHING
OXFORD AND PORTLAND, OREGON
2005

Hart Publishing
Oxford and Portland, Oregon

Published in North America (US and Canada) by
Hart Publishing c/o
International Specialized Book Services
5804 NE Hassalo Street
Portland, Oregon
97213-3644
USA

Hart Publishing is a specialist legal publisher based in Oxford, England.
To order further copies of this book or to request a list of other publications please write to:

Hart Publishing, Salter's Boatyard, Folly Bridge,
Abingdon Road, Oxford OX1 4LB
Telephone: +44 (0)1865 245533 or Fax: +44 (0)1865 794882
e-mail: mail@hartpub.co.uk
WEBSITE: http//www.hartpub.co.uk

British Library Cataloguing in Publication Data
Data Available
ISBN 1–84113–454–6 (paperback)

Typeset by Hope Services (Abingdon) Ltd.

www.bloomsbury.com

PREFACE

This book argues that the European Union is failing adequately to protect consumer's critical interests in e-commerce. It seeks to prove that argument by evidencing a pattern of deficiencies in the protection of those interests and then contrasting that pattern with the EU's close protection of producers' corresponding interests. The contrast discounts the possibilities that the failures in the consumer field are due to general difficulties inherent in harmonising national law or to specific difficulties involved in regulating electronic commerce. The width of the argument together with limited time led inevitably to shallows. Notwithstanding those shallows, I believe that the argument is both made out and valuable. It is valuable in particular because surveys currently show that consumers have little confidence in buying online, and that as a result the potential of e-commerce, a motor of European integration *par excellence*, is not being fulfilled.

This book is based on a PhD thesis written at the University of Warwick and for their support in that area I would like to thank my initial and subsequent supervisors, Chris Willett and Andrew Clark, my external examiners, Lilian Edwards and Geraint Howells, and my internal adviser, Alan Neal.

This book is dedicated to Anna, Jo, and Gordon.

John Dickie
University of Leicester
March 2005

CONTENTS

TABLE OF CASES

European Court of Human Rights

European Court of Justice

TABLE OF INSTRUMENTS

EU Instruments

Directives

EC Treaty

EU Instruments (General)

International Instruments

National Legislation

Australia

France

Germany

Norway

South Africa

United Kingdom

United States

1

Introduction

The Argument

This book seeks to argue that the European Community is failing adequately to protect consumers' critical interests in e-commerce, despite having the practical capability to do so. The issue is an important one from the point of view of the Community because e-commerce is a motor of integration *par excellence*, and Community consumers currently lack confidence in it.[1]

[1] In mid-2003 only 10 per cent of consumers felt that cross-border online shoppers enjoyed a high level of protection within the EU: European Opinion Research Group, *Consumer Protection in the EU*, November 2003, at 10.

Chapters 2–4 below seek to prove the first part of the argument by evidencing a pattern of deficiencies in the Community's protection of consumers' critical interests in e-commerce; Chapters 5–6 seek to prove the second part of the argument by contrasting that pattern of deficiencies with the Community's close protection of producers' corresponding interests (thus are discounted the possibilities that the failures in the consumer field are due to the general difficulties inherent in harmonising national law or the specific difficulties involved in regulating electronic commerce).

The book's hypothesis raises three preliminary issues:

- — what are the specific challenges of e-commerce, as distinct from commerce generally?
- — what are consumers' and producers' 'critical interests'?
- — what is the Community's role in protecting those interests?

These three issues will now be examined in turn.

The Distinctive Nature of E-Commerce

> OECD: 'Electronic commerce refers generally to all forms of commercial transactions involving both organisations and individuals, that are based upon the electronic processing and transmission of data, including text, sound and visual images. It also refers to the effects that the electronic exchange of commercial information may have on the institutions and process that support and govern commercial activities.'[2]

> European Commission: 'Electronic commerce covers mainly two types of activity—the electronic ordering of tangible goods, which still must be physically delivered using traditional channels such as postal services or commercial couriers; and direct electronic commerce—the online ordering, payment and delivery of intangible goods and services such as computer software, entertainment content, or information services on a global scale'.[3]

Whilst e-commerce has been used for many years by closed groups of businesses, modern e-commerce, as the OECD's definition above indicates, is generally open. In particular, it includes within its scope the Internet, which has altered the traditional structure of the marketplace, as Table 1 from the European Commission's *Initiative in Electronic Commerce* shows:

[2] *Electronic Commerce: Opportunities and Challenges for Government* (1997), at 11.
[3] *A European Initiative in Electronic Commerce*, COM(97) 157 at I(7).

TABLE 1[4]: Traditional *vs.* Internet *E-Commerce*

TRADITIONAL E-COMMERCE	*INTERNET* E-COMMERCE
Business to business only	business to consumers business to business business to public administration
Closed 'clubs', often industry-specific	open marketplace, unlimited partners
Closed, proprietary networks	open networks
Known, trusted partners	known and unknown partners
Security part of network design	security and authentication needed
THE MARKET IS A CLUB	**THE NETWORK IS THE MARKET**

The distinctive characteristics of modern e-commerce are based on the technical features of the Internet ('the Net'). The Net is a collection of interconnected computers which support common communications standards (in particular the Transmission Control and Internet Protocols).[5] Its origins lie in 1960s research conducted by the United States into ways of proofing computer systems against nuclear attack by re-routing packets of information if the most direct route was blocked.[6] The influence of these origins is still in evidence today, the Net has a 'distributed architecture', rather than the hierarchical structure of more established mass media, something which makes it inherently more difficult to control. The Net is a 'bottom-up', not a 'top-down' medium, and does not have concentrated points of production as do television, radio, and print (ie in the form of transmitters and presses). The Net has millions of points of production.

The three most important *architects* of the electronic marketplace are the Internet Engineering Task Force (IETF), the World Wide Web Consortium (W3C) and the Internet Corporation for Assigned Names and Numbers (ICANN), and some consideration of their roles is necessary for a proper understanding of the construction of the marketplace.

First, the IETF is responsible for the transfer standards which underlie the Internet's functionality as a global network. The most important are the Transfer Control Protocol/Internet Protocol and the Simple Mail Transfer Protocol. The IETF describes itself as, 'a large open international community

[4] Commission, note 3 above, at I(2).

[5] See generally: K Connor-Sax and E Krol, *The Whole Internet: The Next Generation* (Sebastopol, O'Reilly, 1999) at 14 and following; J Naughton, *A Brief History of the Future: The Origins of the Internet* (Phoenix, 2000).

[6] Indeed the European Community also originated in a fear of war—the founders saw economic and political integration as a means to achieve interdependence and thus peace.

of network designers, operators, vendors, and researchers concerned with the evolution of the Internet architecture and the smooth operation of the Internet. It is open to any interested individual.'[7] Most of its members are software engineers.

The IETF has a history of rivalry with the International Telecommunications Union, whose members represent sovereign countries, and to a large extent, the interests of their respective telecoms companies; this rivalry has been driven by the ITU's fear of competition from Internet telephony and has manifested itself in competing e-mail standards for example.[8]

Second, the W3C is a grouping of 400 member-companies which aims to develop common protocols to ensure the inter-operability of the Web. It was created by Tim Berners-Lee in 1994, and it is now run by three academic institutions—Massachusetts Institute of Technology, the National Institute for Research in Computer Science in France and Keio University in Japan. Its principal achievements have been the Hypertext Transport Protocol (HTTP) and the Hypertext Mark Up Language (HTML). Two of its initiatives in particular will be looked at in the chapters below, namely the Platform for Privacy Preferences in chapter 3 and the Platform Independent Content Selection in chapter 4.

Third, ICANN is, in its own words,

> 'an internationally organized, non-profit corporation that has responsibility for Internet Protocol (IP) address space allocation, protocol identifier assignment, generic (gTLD) and country code (ccTLD) Top-Level Domain name system management, and root server system management functions.'[9]

It was created under a Memorandum of Understanding between the US Department of Commerce and ICANN to manage the transition of the Domain Name System from the US government to the global community; the most recent version of the MoU is intended to be the last and sets out a series of goals for ICANN that are designed to achieve an entirely independent ICANN, although it is not clear exactly when that will happen, and some commentators have been critical of the Department of Commerce's handling of the matter.[10] ICANN's development of a process to resolve disputes over domain names has been controversial and is addressed in detail in chapter 5 below.

[7] http://www.ietf.org/overview.html.

[8] See generally, W Drake, 'The rise and decline of the international telecommunications regime' in C Marsden (ed) *Regulating the Global Information Society* (London, Routledge, 2000) at 162.

[9] http://www.icann.org/general/.

[10] AM Froomkin, 'Wrong Turn in Cyberspace: Using ICANN to Route Around the APA and the Constitution' (2000) 50 *Duke Law Journal* 17.

In practical terms, the Internet is a fast, efficient and global communications medium.[11] The speed and ease of communication possible on the Internet is unrivalled. One survey showed that sending a 42-page document by e-mail from New York to Tokyo took two minutes and cost at most ten US cents (with a possible marginal cost of nil); the next most efficient medium was the fax which took 31 minutes and cost over 28 dollars.[12]

The communications power of the Net allows modern e-commerce to enjoy various advantages over off-line commerce, including low business operating costs and reduced prices for many goods and services. For example, online bookstores typically sell at 40 per cent below high street prices and the cost of a (US) banking transaction on the Internet is $0.01, as against $0.52 using the telephone and $1.07 in a branch.[13] Furthermore, e-commerce offers opportunities for consumers to match corporate power by grouping together.[14]

The extent of Internet use is growing rapidly. Penetration in European homes stood at 42 per cent as at March 2004, and at 90 per cent for businesses and schools.[15] From April 2002 to April 2003, the number of Europeans using high-speed connections (including DSL, LAN and Cable Modem) grew by 136 per cent, with UK experiencing the largest increase at 235 per cent.[16] There is a correlation between high-speed connection and increased use—eg in Germany narrowband users spend on average seven and a half hours on the Web each month, whilst broadband users spend 21.[17]

However, the reputation of the Net as a nirvana for consumers is sometimes inflated: one study which surveyed a wide range of goods available online found that there was a direct price saving in only 15 per cent of the cases, although greater savings were available in the field of services.[18]

[11] Although it should be noted that not all material on the Net is globally accessible in as much as some countries apply restrictions to it. Countries such as Saudi Arabia, for example, oblige all Net service providers to register and route their communications through a single state-run server. Reporteurs Sans Frontières name some forty-five countries which in one way or another restrict citizens' access to the Net, www.rsf.fr/uk/alaune/ennemisweb.html. The Singapore broadcast authorities run a licensing scheme for all those involved in providing content on, or access to, the Net. Licensees are required to use their best efforts to comply with the Code of Practice, which prohibits content such as that which 'propagate permissiveness or promiscuity', 'tend to bring the Government of Singapore into hatred or contempt', or which 'excite disaffection against the Government of Singapore', 'depict or propagate sexual perversions such as homosexuality, lesbianism . . .' See further, www.sba.gov.sg.

[12] WTO, *Electronic Commerce and the Role of the WTO* (1998) at 13.

[13] US Department of Commerce, *The Emerging Digital Economy* (www.ecommerce.gov, 1998) at 26.

[14] See M Kane, 'Prix fixé? Not on the Net' (www.zdnet.co.uk/news/1999/41/ns–10750.html, October 1999), which discusses the growth of consumer-empowering pricing mechanisms such as auctions, reverse auctions, consumer-nominated prices (see eg priceline.com).

[15] COM(2004) 91 at 2.

[16] *Ibid.*

[17] *Ibid.*

[18] Stiftung Warentest, 'Electronic Commerce in Europe' (Berlin, 1999) at 46–51.

The communications power of the Net offers particular potential for the commercialisation of digitised data. There are seemingly constant advances in quality and in efficiency of reproduction and distribution.[19] Music, software, pay-TV, pay-radio, information services and video-on-demand are works that are in considerable demand amongst consumers. These types of material may be called up for one-off display or downloaded with a view to repeated use.[20] Although the capacity of traditional electronic storage media (eg DVDs) is currently growing faster than that of online capacity,[21] the ease of online use presages its future dominance. Within the European Community, pay-TV has long been the principal market for films,[22] and the electronic share of the publishing market is forecast to range between 5 per cent and 15 per cent by the year 2005.[23]

The electronic marketplace involves a wide range of economic actors including manufacturers, retailers and consumers; logistics companies which store and distribute the stock of virtual shops; brokers and searchers which locate particular goods and services; catalogue aggregators providing 'one-stop shops' where buyers can select different products from the cheapest suppliers. E-commerce widens the range of goods and services available to consumers, and increases the size of producers' markets. Items can be modelled and customised before purchase. E-commerce can make shopping easier: purchases may be made 24 hours a day, from home, at work or on the move, and certain services can be delivered online. Buyers gain access to goods and services that were previously beyond their geographical or financial reach; the converse of this is also true, sellers gain access to buyers who were previously beyond their reach. Electronic commerce lowers entry barriers, expands existing markets and creates new markets.

From a legal point of view, the most important practical applications of the Internet are the World Wide Web, e-mail and Usenet:

[19] The cost of buying software via an Internet retailer was estimated by the WTO to average 35 US cents per transaction in 1998, as compared to 15 US dollars via a traditional retailer: WTO, note 12 above, at 14.

[20] As the capacity of both networks and personal computers increases, market growth for original works is likely to accelerate. To give some idea of current network capacity, transmission of the contents of a typical music CD over the Internet from the United States to Europe through the copper-wire telephone network would take approximately seventeen hours.

[21] The recently-developed Digital Versatile Disk has a capacity ten times that of a CD. Online capacity is currently dependent largely on physical lines of communication which are expensive to replace.

[22] 34 per cent of movie spending per consumer, as against 31 per cent in the cinema: Commission, *Proposal for a European Parliament and Council Directive on the Legal Protection of Services based on, or consisting of, Conditional Access*, COM(97) 356 at 5.

[23] Commission, *Proposal for a Directive on copyright in the information society*, COM(1999) 250, at 8.

World Wide Web ('The Web'): The Web is a collection of passive and interactive electronic documents which are accessible throughout the world via the Internet. These documents are made accessible via the use of a Universal Resource Locator or 'Web-site address'—such as *http://www.pepsi.com*—registered on a first-come, first-served basis.[24] Web sites may be entirely passive, simply presenting information, or they may be active in a variety of ways, for example by collecting data from users or displaying advertisements to them (overtly or covertly). In this respect the Web differs from television and radio, for example, which, although forms of mass media, consist almost entirely of one-way communication. From a commercial point of view, the Web is the most important part of the Net.

E-mail: E-mail is electronic messaging, generally of text, transmitted from a sender to one or more recipients. E-mail may be sent to, or received from, a list of people who are interested in a particular topic. There are hundreds of thousands of such lists and often those sending to the list will neither know, nor be able to find out, what addresses are on the list. It should be noted that e-mail and the Web can be used together, for example a Web page may contain a 'form' to be filled in by an individual which is then sent by e-mail.

Usenet: The Usenet is a collection of newsgroups, related to particular interest areas, which contain messages posted by subscribers. As with e-mail lists, those who post messages generally cannot control who will see them. The Usenet has a reputation for facilitating speech which some regard as undesirable, including exchanges of pornography and copyright material.

There are three characteristics of the Net which particularly distinguish it from other communications media—borderlessness, transience and size. These will now be discussed in turn.

Borderlessness

'The geography of the Internet . . . is purely virtual.' *Professor Christopher Reed.*[25]

There is no reliable method of independently verifying the geographical origin of a communication carried over the Net, originating for example from an e-mail or from a 'dot.com' Web address.[26] A Web-site or e-mail may give a prima facie indication of origin through a country code such as '.uk' or '.fr', but this is no guarantee that related communications are emanating from those countries (although some country-code top level domain name registrars do insist that registrants reside within the country). For example, a shop in

[24] This 'address' is a coded form of a unique number which identifies the server on which the information is stored. Those seeking the site enter the address, and the number is then found by a directing service.

[25] *Internet Law: Text and Materials* (London, Butterworths, 2000) at 187.

[26] These applications are discussed further below. '.com' is one of a number of 'generic top level domains' in respect of which there are no restrictions as to who may register names within them. It is designed for commercial organisations.

Germany may maintain a '.uk' Web-site for the purposes of selling to UK consumers, but have no other link whatsoever to the UK.[27] All communications from the site may in fact come from staff outside the UK. The server from which the communications are made may be located anywhere in the world.

A further aspect of the Net's borderlessness is the difficulty of *restricting* communications to particular locations.[28] A communication on a Web-site is prima facie accessible from anywhere in the world.

Transience

'The supplier may hide behind the business seat of the provider . . . He is everywhere and nowhere, a little bit like Alice in Wonderland.' *Professor Norbert Reich.*[29]

The Net's transience is based on the intangible nature of the communications it supports. A Web site able to reach millions of people can be set up, moved or closed down in minutes, leaving little or no trace of its prior existence.[30] This transience includes the potential for anonymity granted by the Net.[31] Little or no verified identity is usually required to establish an e-mail account or Web-site. There are services which are specifically designed to give users anonymous access to e-mail.[32] Once established, the identity of the sender or owner can usually be masked.[33]

27 J-P Robé has pointed out the contrast with the off-line world, in which it has traditionally been important to be close to factors of production: 'Multinational Enterprises: The Constitution of a Pluralistic Legal Order', in G Teubner, *Global Law Without a State* (Aldershot, Dartmouth, 1997) at 45.

28 Although, as pointed out in the French *Yahoo!* case, content providers can block 90 per cent of users based in a particular country by identifying the server through which they are given access (*Association Union Des Etudiants Juifs de France and Ligue Contre le Racisme et l'Antisemitisme c/ Yahoo! Inc. et Yahoo! France,* Tribunal de Grande Instance de Paris, Ordonnance de référé du 22 May 2000, *Electronic Commerce & Law Report,* 14/6/00 at 647). Sites can of course ask users to identify their location, but this method is reliant on users' honesty.

29 'Consumerism and citizenship in the Information Society—The Case of Electronic Contracting', in T Wilhelmsson and others, *Consumer Law in the Information Society* (Kluwer Law International, The Hague, 2001) 163 at 168.

30 For an analysis of the problems this can cause within the legal process, see S Benjamin, 'Stepping into the same river twice: rapidly changing facts and the appellate process', (1999) 78(2) *Texas Law Review* 273, also www.acusd.edu/~stuarb/article.html.

31 See for a general discussion of relevant technical matters, Commission Working Party on Data Protection Recommendation 3/97, *Anonymity on the Internet* (www.europa.eu.int/comm/internalmarket/en/media/dataprot/index.htm).

32 See eg www.freedom.net.

33 Either by inserting a false identity in the 'From:' header, or by using software specifically designed to alter identifying information, or by using a remailer such as www.anonymizer.com. This service can also be used to 'anonymise' visits to Web-sites.

Size

The Net is huge. In 2003 one survey reported over 40 million Web sites in existence world-wide.[34] *Ebay's* auction site has at any one time approximately 1 million items for sale and theoretically anyone in the world could buy them. This point is significant from the point of view of transnational commerce, ie the *nature* of the problems associated with electronic commerce are similar to those associated with traditional forms of distant commerce such as mail order. However, the size of the Net (combined with its borderlessness and transience) greatly increases the *scale* of the problems.

The Current Economic Context of E-Commerce in the Community

As at 2003, 70 per cent of EU companies had their own website,[35] whilst between 2000 and 2002 Internet penetration in EU households moved from 18 per cent to 43 per cent.[36] The development of broadband and multiplatform access (ie via means other than a PC, such as a mobile phone or TV) has given fresh impetus to growth. Currently, e-commerce accounts for only 1–2 per cent of retail sales in the EU, and only 12 per cent of enterprises are selling online,[37] but the sector is growing—online Christmas shopping grew by 86 per cent between 2002 and 2003.[38] In 2003, only 13 per cent of Europeans shopped in another European country, with 23 per cent of relevant purchases being made online.[39]

Evidence of increasing online advertising is further evidence of the likely future growth of e-commerce. In the UK for example, advertising in the form of banners, pop-ups, and keywords[40] increased 52 per cent between 2001 and 2002, whilst in France it more than doubled (from 153 million euros to 309 million).[41] Online advertising has various advantages over its more traditional counterparts, in particular the facility quickly to tailor advertising to the particular interests of individual consumers via online identification.

Online advertising is not always geared towards generating online purchases, rather it can be used to give information on goods and services which are bought elsewhere. Concrete statistics on the extent of such pre-sale use of

[34] Netcraft Web Server Survey, http://news.netcraft.com/archives/2003/07/index.html.

[35] European E-business Report 2002/2003, www.e-business-watch.org.

[36] Report from the Commission on Directive 2000/31 on e-commerce, COM(2003) 702 final at 4.

[37] COM(2003) 702 at 5.

[38] COM(2003) 702 at 5.

[39] European Opinion Research Group, note 1 above, at 5.

[40] Ie the response-list positions which search engines sell to producers.

[41] Interactive Advertising Bureau UK, 'Europe's marketer's switch to on-line', June 2003.

the Internet are not available although surveys indicate that such usage is significant.[42]

Consumer confidence varies across the EU, with particular variations in perception as to protection at home and abroad. In relation to consumer protection generally, whilst 48 per cent of all Europeans in 2003 believed that they had a high level of consumer protection at home, only 20 per cent believed the same applied to them when shopping in other EU countries.[43] In relation to e-commerce, these figures were reduced respectively to 22 per cent and 10 per cent.[44]

Summary of the Distinctive Nature of E-Commerce

The characteristics outlined above combine to make the Net a unique communications medium. Television and radio share some of the Net's characteristics of transience and size, but are generally bordered, non-interactive, and emanate from single rather than multiple sources.[45] The telephone, fax and mail transcend national borders, but do not have the capacity of the Net. Print can be an anonymous mass medium, but is more permanent than the Net and does not have the latter's capacity for interaction.

Having justified the treatment of e-commerce as a distinct field of commerce generally, the question of consumers' and producers' critical interests therein will now be addressed.

Defining 'Consumers', 'Producers' and the Notion of 'Critical Interests'

This book focuses on the relationship between 'producers'[46] acting in the course of business, and 'consumers'[47] acting outside the course of business.

[42] See Doubleclick, 'Touchpoints: Effective Marketing Sequences in the Interactive Media Age', www.doubleclick.com/us/knowledge, March 2003.

[43] European Opinion Research Group, note 1 above, at 5.

[44] European Opinion Research Group, note 1 above, at 10.

[45] Compare *ACLU v Reno* 929 F. Supp. 830, (www.aclu.org/court/cdadec.html), in which the United States Supreme Court contradicted the US Government's arguments that the right to free speech on the Net is qualified in the same way it is in the context of broadcast media, pointing out that the Net is not as 'invasive' as radio or television, and that it is not a 'scarce commodity' as is broadcast spectrum. Print and broadcast media have traditionally been regulated in different ways in the West, the latter being subject to licensing, the former generally not (although the first printing presses were licensed, see E Eisenstein, *The Printing Press as Agent of Change: Communications and Cultural Transformation* (Cambridge University Press, 1980).

[46] Ie those natural or legal persons who produce goods and services (including selling).

[47] Ie those natural persons who consume goods and services. Of course, the market might be argued to benefit if legal persons were to be included in this definition, but including them would

The reason why this type of relationship is singled out for special attention is that it generally involves an inequality of relevant resources, which, if unchecked, has the capacity to damage consumer confidence. (It is interesting to contrast the above producer-consumer paradigm with the 'original' paradigm of commerce in primordial times, namely that of barter between two people of roughly equal bargaining power within a close-knit community.)[48]

Consumers and producers can only reasonably expect their *legitimate* interests to be protected and this book takes a deontological, ie moral, approach to the construction of such legitimacy.

The term 'critical interests' refers to the interests which are critical to *confidence* in e-commerce. Whilst factors of confidence are inherently difficult to quantify with precision, the sections below use empirical evidence to identify those interests as far as possible.

Consumers' Critical Interests

Evidence of the interests critical to consumer confidence can be found in a number of empirical surveys of consumer opinion. Two major surveys were carried out in 2000, one by the National Consumer Council[49] and one by the Bertelsmann Foundation.[50] The NCC survey found that:

— most consumers considered the Internet the 'riskiest' of all forms of commerce,[51]
— consumers saw as significant disadvantages to shopping online the need to release credit card details, and the risk of encountering fraudulent suppliers,[52]
— 32 per cent of consumers with Internet access identified lack of privacy as one of the main disadvantages of online shopping.[53]

The Bertelsmann survey found that:

to some extent run counter to the rationale for consumer protection cited above, as well as cause grave problems to producers' ability to determine who is and who is not a 'consumer'.

[48] From an English point of view, it is further interesting to note that the parity of bargaining power within the 'primordial' paradigm was mirrored in the nineteenth-century mercantile disputes which drove the development of much modern contract law.

[49] National Consumer Council, *E-commerce and consumer protection*, (www.ncc.org.uk), at 3 and 5. The survey consisted of discussion groups and of a structured questionnaire answered by 2100 households across Great Britain.

[50] Bertelsmann Foundation, *Internet User Survey* (www.stiftung.bertelsmann.de/internet content/english/content/c3200.htm) at 15.

[51] At 3. Consumer risk in e-commerce is also intuitively obvious, ie consumers are physically removed from both goods and producers, and must generally pay for goods before receiving them.

[52] At 5. The survey found that whilst 26 per cent of the UK adult population had access to the Internet either at home or at work, only 3 per cent regularly shopped online.

[53] At 25.

— consumers considered 'privacy' to be 'the major risk' of using the Net,[54]
— pornography was considered the second 'major risk' of the Net (children being singled out as a special concern), and a majority of those surveyed wanted to see pornographic and racist material blocked.[55]

Other surveys have echoed these results. *A Eurobarometer* survey conducted in the early days of e-commerce found that two-thirds of consumers were concerned about the trails of personal data they leave on information networks.[56] The Internet Watch Foundation's Report *Internet Content Rating for Europe* 2000,[57] found that 'serious concerns' were expressed by 70 per cent of Internet-users about violent content, and by 74 per cent about erotic content.[58] A study by Childnet International and Fleishman Hillard in 2000 found concern amongst European consumers regarding the availability to children of pornographic, racist, hate and violent material online, as well as the risks of children meeting paedophiles through chat-rooms,[59] and anxiety that children had greater technical knowledge of the Internet than adults did.[60] (Similar concerns can be found outside Europe—in one US survey 87 per cent of respondents stated that they were somewhat, or very, concerned about threats to their privacy online.)[61]

The surveys above demonstrate that consumers attach particular importance to their interests in 'fair trading', 'privacy' and 'morality'. The latter is largely a proxy interest, ie held by parents on behalf of children, yet it can nevertheless be powerful in hampering consumer use of e-commerce. Children are de facto buyers of goods and users of services, and much of the potential of e-commerce lies in its facilitation of home-shopping—yet parents may be discouraged from allowing this (some even perhaps from installing Internet access) whilst the electronic environment is not safe for children. It is clear that computer use amongst children is very common—one recent survey covering Denmark, Ireland, Sweden, Norway and Iceland found that 97 per cent of children aged 9 to 16 years had used a computer.[62] The link between commercial confidence and protection of morality has been recognised by the Parliament and the Council:

[54] At 3.
[55] At 4 and 15.
[56] 'Information Technology and Data Protection' (1997) *Eurobarometer* at 46.1.
[57] http://www.ispo.cec.be/iap/decision/en.html, April 2000.
[58] At 23.
[59] 'Promoting safe use of the Internet', www.netaware.org/home/finalEUreport.pdf (no longer available), 2000, at 4–6.
[60] *Ibid*, at 4.
[61] FTC, *Self-Regulation and Privacy Online: A Federal Trade Commission Report to Congress* (http://www.ftc.gov/os/1999/9907/index.htm#13, July 1999).
[62] COM(2004) 91 at 3.

> '. . . the amount of harmful and illegal content carried over the Internet, while limited, could adversely affect the establishment of the necessary favourable environment for initiatives and undertakings to flourish; whereas it is essential, in order to ensure that consumers make full use of the Internet, that a safer environment for its use is created . . .'[63]

Furthermore, there may be in process a 'delayed' reduction in confidence, given the time it takes for parents to catch up with the reality of their children's experiences online—the Commission's 2004 Proposal for a Decision on promoting safer use of the Internet reports that whilst 30 per cent of children have seen Web sites with violent material, only 15 per cent of parents think their children have done so, and that whilst 14 per cent of them have met someone they first met online, only 4 per cent of parents think they have done this.[64]

The nature of the three interests identified above will now be broken down.

I—Fair Trading

Consumers' fair trading interest is postulated as that in adequate information about producers and products,[65] secure payment mechanisms, and redress where a product does not meet their reasonable expectations. (This book will not focus sharply on the general questions surrounding the nature of consumers' reasonable expectations as to product quality, those questions are not specific to e-commerce and the general Community position has been dealt with elsewhere at length.)[66] The legitimacy of the fair trading interest derives from the fact that consumer participation in the marketplace is predicated upon a belief that the interest will be respected, and thus producers, through the very nature of their activity, can be taken implicitly to accept it.[67]

[63] *Decision 276/1999/EC of the European Parliament and of the Council adopting a multi-annual action plan on promoting safer use of the Internet*, Recitals (2) and (3), (http://158.169.50.95:10080/legal/en/iap/index.html).

[64] COM(2004) 91, at 3.

[65] See generally: J Stiglitz, 'The Contributions of the Economics of Information to Twentieth-Century Economics' (2000) *Quarterly Journal of Economics* 1441; G Hadfield *et al*, 'Information-Based Principles for Rethinking Consumer Protection Policy' (1998) 21 *Journal of Consumer Policy* 131.

[66] See especially: H Beale and G Howells, 'EC Harmonisation of Consumer Sales Law—A missed opportunity?' (1997) 12 *Journal of Contract Law* 21; R Bradgate and C Twigg-Flesner, 'The EC Directive On Certain Aspects of the Sale of Consumer Goods and Associated Guarantees—All Talk and No Do?' [2000] 2 *Web Journal of Current Legal Issues* (http://webjcli.ncl.ac.uk/2000/contents2.html); J Lowry and D Oughton, 'Consumer Law into the Next Millennium: A Serious Service Fault' in D Hayton (ed) *Law's Futures* (Oxford, Hart, 2000).

[67] See generally on consumer confidence as a necessary part of a successful marketplace: H-W Micklitz, 'Principles of Justice in Private Law within the European Union' in E Paasivirta and K Rissanen (eds), *Principles of Justice within the European Union* (European Commission DGXIII, 1996).

II—Privacy

Consumers' privacy interest is postulated as that in individuals having control over their personal data. That control can be broken down chronologically into the need for consent to collection in relation to nominated purposes, for access to data once collected, and for the security of data. The legitimacy of the interest lies in a conceptualisation of privacy as an aspect of human autonomy—as part of 'the inviolate personality, the individual's independence, dignity and integrity', in the words of Bloustein.[68]

III—Morality

From the studies discussed above it can be seen that consumers' morality interest in the context of e-commerce is most concerned with the need to protect children from online material which is explicitly sexual or violent and, to a lesser extent in quantitative terms, the need to protect children using chat-rooms from sexual predators. The legitimacy of the second interest is obvious. The legitimacy of the first interest stems from the damage which explicitly sexual or violent material can cause to children, given their propensity to mimic. (The causal link between such material and damage is inherently difficult to prove because of the ethical problems which would be associated with related experiments.)

Producers' Critical Interests

There are no surveys of producer confidence in e-commerce comparable to those cited above in relation to consumer confidence—there would appear to be no general problem with producer confidence. The most important interest of producers is of course that of payment, and this interest is easily protected by payment being taken before supply. As regards those interests which producers cannot protect through such 'self-help', a number of arguments support the identification of the interests in authorship and in domain-identity as being of particular importance to producers' confidence in e-commerce; those arguments are:

[68] E Bloustein, 'Privacy as an Aspect of Human Dignity' (1964) 39 *New York University Law Review* 902 at 971. Expressed by L Velecky as the right of an individual to be 'captain of his soul'—'The Concept of Privacy', in J Young (ed), *Privacy* (John Wiley & Sons, Chichester, 1978) at 31.

— in respect of the authorship interest, that, (a) demand for original work is very large,[69] and (b) the Internet offers unique possibilities for unauthorised copying and re-using of, and access to, original work;[70]
— in respect of the domain-identity interest, that consumers' ability easily to establish contact with producers is the latter's very lifeblood in the electronic marketplace, and the current system of unique domain names, together with the ephemeral nature of the Internet, can hamper easy contact (for reasons discussed in chapter 6 below).

Support for the above interests as being those critical to producer confidence online comes from relevant statements of producers[71] and (within the framework of existing law) the law reports, ie litigation.[72] The nature of the interests will now be discussed.

I—Authorship

Producers' authorship interest is postulated as that in securing the online fruit of their original work. (This book's unitary approach to the concept of 'producers' conflates the otherwise separable interests of authors and distributors of original work.)[73] The legitimacy of the authorship interest stems from producers' moral claim to that fruit.

II—Domain-identity

Producers' domain-identity interest is that in securing the online fruit of their identity, ie enabling consumers easily to locate them and their products. This will typically focus on whether consumers can use the name of a producer or product as the root of a domain name, eg pepsi.com, toyota.co.uk, etc. The legitimacy of the interest stems from producers' moral claim to the fruit of their identity.

[69] See chapter 5 below.
[70] *Ibid.*
[71] See for example the Working Group on Intellectual Property of the Global Business Dialogue on electronic commerce (http://www.gbde.org/structure/working/ipr.html).
[72] In relation to authorship interests, see eg: *Shetland Times v Wills* [1997] FSR 604, and other cases cited in chapter 5 below. In relation to the domain-identity interest, see eg: *British Telecommunications plc v One in a Million Ltd* [1998] All ER 476 (www.nic.uk/news/oiam-appeal-judgement.html), and other cases cited in chapter 6 below.
[73] This interest is recognised by the Universal Declaration of Human Rights: 'Everyone has the right to the protection of the moral and material interests resulting from any scientific, literary or artistic production of which he is the author' (Article 27(1)).

The Role of the European Community

'Cyberspace'—Is there a Role for Public Regulation At All?

Some commentators have questioned whether *any* public and bordered entity can properly claim competence in governing 'borderless' online activity:

> 'Global computer-based communications cut across territorial borders, creating a new realm of human activity and undermining the feasibility—and legitimacy—of applying laws based on geographic boundaries. While these electronic communications play havoc with geographic boundaries, a new boundary, made up of the screens and passwords that separate the virtual world from the 'real world' of atoms, emerges. This new boundary defines a distinct Cyberspace that needs and can create new law and legal institutions of its own. Territorially-based law-making and law-enforcing authorities find this new environment deeply threatening. But established territorial authorities may yet learn to defer to the self-regulatory efforts of Cyberspace participants who care most deeply about this new digital trade in ideas, information and services.' *Professors David Johnson and David Post.*[74]

Johnson and Post's argument as to the *illegitimacy* of public regulators claiming jurisdiction over 'global' electronic communications can be seen as false in that all so-called 'global' communications are local to the places where the sender and receiver are located. It has long been accepted in the Community and elsewhere in case-law, legislation and theory that a sovereign can legitimately claim personal jurisdiction over an actor located outside its borders in cases where the actor behaves in such a way that substantially impacts within those borders.[75]

Further, it is *feasible* for public regulators such as the Community to claim jurisdiction over 'global' electronic communications. First, the actors involved will in many cases be within the Community's jurisdiction, and thus there subject to the standard powers of enforcement of law. Even where the actor is

[74] D Johnson and D Post, 'Law and Borders—The Rise of Law in Cyberspace' (1996) 48 *Stanford Law Review* 1367 (www.cli.org/X0025_LBFIN.html) at 1. See also: JP Barlow, 'A Cyber space Declaration of Independence' (www.eff.org, 1996); J Delacourt, 'The International Impact of Internet Regulation' (1997) 38 *Harvard International Law Journal* 207; F Boyle, 'Foucault in Cyberspace: Surveillance, Sovereignty and Hardwired Censors' (1997) 66 *University of Cincinatti Law Review* 1777. The OECD has referred to self-regulation as the 'Brave New World' model, *Gateways to the Global Market: Consumer and Electronic Commerce* (March 1997) at 25.

[75] See eg: Article 13(3)(a) of Council Regulation 44/2001 on Jurisdiction and Enforcement of Judgments in Civil and Commercial Matters, which provides for jurisdiction over consumer contracts to lie with the courts of the consumer's state of domicile where the conclusion of the contract was preceded by a specific invitation addressed to him or by advertising. (See also the parallel US doctrine of 'minimum contacts': *International Shoe Co. v Washington*, 326 US 310, 316 (1945).)

outside the jurisdiction, this does not mean it is unfeasible for the Community to claim jurisdiction. Foreign enforcement of a judgement may be available, or the actor may have assets within the jurisdiction which can be attached.

Whilst the argument of Johnson and Post is superficially attractive, most commentators now accept that new electronic communications media do not constitute a realm of activity outside the scope of legitimate public regulation.[76]

The Potential of 'Self-help'

Whilst the general thrust of the argument of Johnson and Post above is false, they are right to point out the advantages of self-help in the electronic environment. The Community can only justify action where economic actors themselves cannot achieve the desired objective, as has been recognised by the European Commission's first guiding principle of Community regulation of e-commerce—'No regulation for regulation's sake.'[77] In analysing the potential of self-help, Larry Lessig's threefold classification of non-law regulation—norms, markets and architecture—can usefully be adopted.[78]

Norms commonly stop people behaving in such a way that will bring the opprobrium of others. For example, those who send off-topic messages to discussion lists may be ejected from them and those who send junk e-mail can find that offended recipients electronically attack their computer systems.[79] Groups of traders may establish sets of standards which they promise to abide by.[80] The potential there exists for specific user-groups to make rules to govern themselves, and for rapid and economical dispute resolution. However, in an online commercial context norms may not be as powerful as they are offline. In particular, the opprobrium of the Internet 'community' may not have

[76] See for example: C Reed, *Internet Law: Text and Material* (London, Butterworths, 2000), describing Johnson and Post's scenario as a 'cyberspace fallacy', at 1; J Goldsmith, 'Against Cyberanarchy' (1998) 65 *University of Chicago Law Review* 1199.

[77] Commission, note 3 above, at III(2).

[78] L Lessig, *Code: and other laws of cyberspace* (New York, Basic Books, 1999), at 88 and following.

[79] Although these 'attacks' are seldom effective, as senders usually use 'disposable' e-mail addresses. See generally, L Edwards, 'Canning the Spam: Is There a Case for Legal Control of Junk Electronic Mail?' in L Edwards and C Waelde (eds), *Law and the Internet* (Oxford, Hart Publishing, 2000) at 313. It has been argued that the Internet community might develop a set of norms similar to the Law Merchant—the rules which mediaeval traders themselves developed in the light of their own expertise and needs, Johnston and Post, note 27 above, at III; see generally, H Mertens, 'Lex Mercatoria: A self-applying system beyond national law?' in Teubner, note 27 above. However, the parallel is not exact, in particular the Law Merchant governed relations between small numbers of actors who were known to one another, that situation is not reproduced in the electronic marketplace.

[80] Examples are discussed in particular in the chapters on consumer protection and privacy below.

the same negative effects as the opprobrium of more tightly-knit, physical communities.[81]

Markets regulate through price and availability. The price of access to the Internet regulates the ability of economic actors to use it, and the price of goods and services sold online regulates consumers' ability to buy. Market forces are not *exceptional* in the context of the Internet, as the price of access to the Internet is not high in relation to the disposable income of most Europeans,[82] and goods and services are generally at least as cheap as they are offline. However, market forces are not unimportant, for example the price and availability of privacy-protecting software will necessarily condition its potential in protecting consumers.

Finally, *architecture* regulates the online community. The technical structure of the Internet regulates the economic actors operating within it. The Internet is dependent upon common communications standards, which allow and disallow certain actions. For example, they allow Web-sites to place identifying files on users' computers but do not allow absolute *restrictions* on communications to particular geographic locations.[83]

Chapters 2 to 6 below take norms, markets and architecture into account in assessing the extent to which self-help is capable of protecting consumers' and producers' critical interests, and then go on to investigate the extent to which the Community fills any gaps. The background to such Community action will now be addressed, followed by an assessment of its legal competence.

Background to Community Activity

> 'The development of information society services within [the EU] . . . is vital to eliminating the barriers which divide the European peoples.' *Recital 1 to Directive 2000/31/EC on e-commerce.*

The Community's first major initiative in the field of e-commerce came in 1997 with the Commission Communication *A European Initiative in Electronic Commerce*.[84] It argued generally that the high levels of technological penetration in Europe created fertile conditions for the electronic marketplace,[85] and clearly envisaged the regulatory focus as lying beyond the Member States, stating that the EU must ensure that:

[81] Of course the contrary may be the case where e-mail lists and newsgroups are used, but in respect of rogue traders, such communications forums will not always be effective in warning consumers of them.

[82] Indeed in the UK it is offered free by public libraries.

[83] See chapter 2 below and page 13 above respectively.

[84] Note 3 above.

[85] As an example of the high level of technological penetration it cites the remarkable fact that more people have access to the Internet in the Netherlands than in the United States: Commission, note 3 above, at I(19).

> 'a coherent regulatory framework for electronic commerce is created at European level. Such a regulatory framework will inevitably be built on existing Single Market legislation which already creates the right conditions for online businesses.'[86]

The Communication set out four guiding principles for this European regulatory framework:

> '1. No regulation for regulation's sake: in many cases, the free movement of electronic commerce services can be effectively achieved by mutual recognition of national rules and of appropriate self-regulatory codes. This means that companies engaged in cross-border business operate under the law of the country of origin ('home country control'). Only where mutual recognition does not suffice to remove obstacles in the market or to protect general interest objectives, will there be a need for Community action. Any legislative action should impose the fewest possible burdens on the market and keep pace with market developments.
>
> 2. Any regulation must be based on all Single Market freedoms: electronic commerce cuts across a wide range of cross-border activities. Whether companies engaged in electronic commerce are providing one or several goods and/or services, freedom to do so—easily and effectively—must be at the heart of future policies. Equal weight must be given to all the freedoms offered by the Single Market: the realisation of the free movement of goods, persons, services and capital together with the freedom of establishment. Only in this way can the crucial objectives of coherence, predictability and operational simplicity be achieved.
>
> 3. Any regulation must take account of business realities: in any electronic commerce operation, a trader needs to set up business, to promote its products or services and to sell, deliver and finance them. This is part of the normal process of trading—a commercial chain. In many cases, legislation will not be necessary to tackle actual or potential problems. Where it is, it must seek to facilitate operations throughout the commercial chain, for it makes no sense to remove barriers in only one part of that chain whilst leaving others untouched.
>
> 4. Any regulation must meet general interest objectives effectively and efficiently: a Single Market for electronic commerce will not develop without the effective safeguarding of recognised general interest objectives such as privacy or consumer protection and other public interests such as wide accessibility to the networks. Without such protection there is a real risk that national regulatory borders will remain in place as individual Member States seek to safeguard the reasonable concerns of their citizens.'[87]

The following chapters will assess the extent to which these principles have been applied. A year after its *European Initiative in Electronic Commerce*, the Commission addressed general *external* issues in a further Communication,

[86] Commission, note 3 above, at III(38).

[87] Commission, note 3 above, at III–2. See also, Commission Communication, *eEurope, An Information Society for all*, COM(1999) 812

Globalisation and the Information Society—The Need for Strengthened International Co-ordination.[88] This document followed the strands of its predecessor in stressing the potential benefits of the information society to Europe, but focused primarily on the global arena, arguing for an International Charter, which would:

— be a multi-lateral understanding on a method of coordination to remove obstacles for the global electronic marketplace;
— be legally non-binding;
— recognise the work of existing international organisations;
— promote the participation of private sector and relevant social groups;
— contribute to more regulatory fair trading.[89]

Although no such Charter has yet emerged, the Commission's emphasis on the importance of an international focus has been maintained, as is discussed in the section below.

The Community in a Global Context

> '. . . the legal framework supporting commercial transactions on the Internet should be governed by consistent principles across state, national, and international borders that lead to predictable results regardless of the jurisdiction in which a particular seller or buyer resides.' *US President Clinton and Vice-President Gore, A Framework for Electronic Commerce.*[90]

The gap between the potential and the reality of e-commerce is not limited to the Community context, rather it is global. However, the global marketplace has no law-making machinery comparable to that of the Community, the largest single market in the industrialised world. Yet it should not be thought thus that the Community operates as an island. Rather, there is a continuous two-way exchange of ideas across its external borders. Its laws are commonly looked to as a model by a number of third countries. The provisions of the Directive on e-commerce relating to intermediary liability, for example, have been closely followed in the South African Electronic Communications and Transactions Act 25 of 2002.[91] (It should be noted that the extra-territorial influence of Community law is not an e-commerce specific phenomenon—the Directive on Product Liability is a good early example of such.)[92] This

88 COM (98) 50.

89 At 3.3.

90 www.whitehouse.gov/eleccomm.htm, 1997, at 3.

91 Government Gazette of the Republic of South Africa (Cape Town 446/23708), 2 August 2002.

92 See D Harland, 'Some reflections on the influence outside Europe of the EC Directive on product liability,' in L Kramer, H Micklitz and K Tonner (eds), *Law and Diffuse Interests in the European Legal Order: Liber Amicorum Norbert Reich* (Baden-Baden, Nomos Verlagsgesellschaft, 1997) 681.

influence can be attributed to three factors. First, the size of the Community as a marketplace for third countries' goods and services. It currently consists of almost 500 million citizens, and is likely to expand in the future.[93] Furthermore, most of its market law is extended to the three additional countries within the European Economic Area, namely Norway, Iceland, Liechtenstein. The second factor in the external influence of Community law is the linkage between the Member States and their ex-colonies, and the third factor is that Community laws are specifically designed to fit differing legal systems and cultures.

In terms of the Commission's participation in global regulation, the OECD and the WTO stand out as particularly important examples, both of which have emphasised the need for international regulatory coordination. The OECD recognised the growing commercial importance of new communications media with the publication in 1997 of its *Electronic Commerce: Opportunities and Challenges for Government*.[94] This Report identified five important areas in relation to governance of e-commerce: first, that governments should reform their regulatory practices to ensure support for the newly liberalised global e-marketplace; second, that existing laws be clarified and where necessary reformed; third, that international agreement on policing and enforcement of laws be pursued; fourth, that the scope, nature and international coherence of intellectual property rights be reviewed; fifth, that discriminatory taxation be avoided (and related solutions be found based on the source and destination of products, and residency of companies).[95] A year after the publication of the Report the OECD hosted a ministerial conference in Ottawa, leading to its *OECD Action Plan for Electronic Commerce*.[96] The Action Plan established a framework for OECD activity in the fields of privacy, consumer protection,[97] communications security, taxation, and access, and activities are ongoing in those areas.[98]

The WTO also stressed the importance of recognising the global nature of e-commerce in its 1998 report, *Electronic Commerce and the Role of the WTO*,[99] arguing that e-commerce will stimulate international trade and produce gains for buyers in quality and price. It identified the principal policy challenges of e-commerce as:

[93] Current candidate countries are Bulgaria, Croatia, Romania and Turkey: www.europa.eu.int/comm/enlargement/index.htm.

[94] The 'Sacher Report' (www.oecd.org/dsti/pubs/sacher.htm).

[95] At 16–17.

[96] Paris, October 1998.

[97] The OECD has subsequently adopted its *Guidelines for Consumer Protection in the Context of Electronic Commerce*, see further, chapter 2 below.

[98] See further, www.oecd.org/subject/e_commerce/.

[99] Paris, WTO.

(i) providing legal and jurisdictional predictability,
(ii) promoting access to this infrastructure,
(iii) securing adequate telecommunications infrastructure and standards,
(iv) ensuring security and privacy of information,
(v) designing appropriate regulation and tax regimes, and
(vi) fostering equal opportunity through appropriate policies to promote education and access, particularly in developing countries.[100]

The Report identified a role for the WTO in facilitating the liberalisation of telecommunications, information technology, public procurement and services, as well as ensuring the protection of intellectual property within the framework of the TRIPS agreement.[101] The WTO has ongoing e-commerce work programmes in relation to facilitating access, reduction of customs duties, and enhancing electronic public procurement.[102]

Current Community Competence in the Field of E-Commerce

> 'Community law and the characteristics of the Community legal order are a vital asset to enable European citizens and operators to take full advantage . . . of the opportunities offered by electronic commerce.' *Recital 3 to Directive 2000/31 on e-commerce.*

The Community does not have universal competence but only that which is attributed to it:

> 'The Community shall act within the limits of the powers conferred upon it by this Treaty and of the objectives assigned to it therein . . .' (Article 5 EC).

Article 14(1) EC imposes upon the Community a duty to adopt measures with the aim of progressively establishing the internal market:

> 'The Community shall adopt measures with the aim of progressively establishing the internal market . . . (2) The internal market shall comprise an area without internal frontiers in which the free movement of goods, persons, services and capital is ensured in accordance with the provisions of the Treaty . . .'[103]

[100] At 69.

[101] At 69. The TRIPS agreement entered into force in 1995, although countries have been given varying transitional periods to comply—the final deadline is 1 January 2006 (for least-developed countries).

[102] See further, www.wto.org/wto/ecom/ecom.htm.

[103] See also Article 95 EC: 'The Council shall, acting in accordance with the procedure referred to in Article 251 and after consulting the Economic and Social Committee, adopt the measures for the approximation of the provisions laid down by law, regulation or administrative action in Member States which have as their object the establishment and functioning of the internal market.' It should be noted that the Community has traditionally taken an expansive view of the legislative competence granted by the enabling provisions within the Treaty. See for example Directive 85/577 on Doorstep Selling, adopted under Article 100 as internal market legislation—harmonisation of door-to-door sales law can hardly be regarded as central to the development of

Given that e-commerce is a motor of the internal market *par excellence*, measures which encourage consumers and producers to participate fully in e-commerce clearly contribute to the progressive establishment of the internal market. This point is recognised in the Preamble to the Directive on e-commerce:

> 'The development of information society services within the Community is hampered by a number of legal obstacles to the proper functioning of the internal market which makes less attractive the exercise of the freedom of establishment and the freedom to provide services; these obstacles arise from divergences in legislation and from the legal uncertainty as to which national rules apply to such services . . .'[104]

E-commerce is a field of shared competence between the Community and the Member States,[105] and thus subject to the test of subsidiarity in the second paragraph of Article 5:

> 'In areas which do not fall within its exclusive competence, the Community shall take action, in accordance with the principle of subsidiarity, only if and insofar as the objectives of the proposed action cannot be sufficiently achieved by the Member States and can therefore, by reason of the scale or effects of the proposed action, be better achieved by the Community.'[106]

Whilst e-commerce is a field of shared competence, its pan-European nature dictates that the Community will often be in a better position than the Member States to regulate it. Once general competence to regulate e-commerce is accepted, then it can be asked what types of action the Community might adopt to support consumer and producer confidence. First, it might support producer and consumer self-help, a role which can be argued to be general to

the single market. Contrast, however, Cases C–376/98 and C–74/99 *Germany v European Parliament and Council* (www.curia.eu.int/en/ep/cp00/aff/cp0072en.htm), in which the Court did strike down Directive 98/43 on Tobacco Advertising because it was founded on an unsuitable legal base (internal market base, whilst the Court held its real objective was public health).

104 Directive 2000/31/EC, Recital 5.

105 The fields of shared and exclusive competence are nowhere officially enumerated (compare the draft Constitutional Treaty, discussed in P Craig, 'Competence: clarity, conferral, containment and consideration' (2004) 29 *European Law Review* 323–44), however e-commerce is a specific part of commerce generally and the Member States certainly have general competence to act in the field of commerce in so far as their actions do not establish barriers to the internal market. See generally on the issue of competence: U di Fabio, 'Some remarks on the Allocation of Competences between the European Union and its Member States' (2002) 39 *Common Market Law Review* 1289.

106 It should be noted that a number of commentators have argued that Article 5 is not in fact a significant limit to the Community's competence: N Emiliou, 'Subsidiarity: An Effective Barrier Against the 'Enterprises of Ambition'?' (1992) 17 *European Law Review* 383. See generally, G de Búrca, 'Reappraising Subsidiarity's Significance after Amsterdam', Jean Monnet Working Paper 7/1999, www.jeanmonnetprogram/org.

public regulation of global commerce.[107] Second, it might provide substantive protection for the threatened interests of consumers and producers, including ensuring that such protection is effective across national borders. The Treaty makes express provision for the Community to take action to ensure that rights can be vindicated across national borders:

> 'Measures in the field of judicial co-operation in civil matters having cross-border implications, to be taken in accordance with Article 67 and insofar as necessary for the proper functioning of the internal market, shall include:
>
> (a) improving and simplifying:
> — the system for cross-border service of judicial and extra-judicial documents;
> — cooperation in the taking of evidence;
> — the recognition and enforcement of decisions in civil and commercial cases, including decisions in extrajudicial cases;
>
> (b) promoting the compatibility of the rules applicable in the Member States concerning the conflict of laws and of jurisdiction . . .' (Article 65 EC).

The qualifications for action under Article 65 above relating to 'cross-border implications' and the 'proper functioning of the internal market'—(these two qualifications were not present in the previous parallel provision of the Third Pillar of the EU Treaty and were apparently included at the behest of the British delegation)[108]—are clearly satisfied in the context of e-commerce.

Whilst Articles 14 and 65 relate to measures in support of the *internal* market, e-commerce is a global phenomenon and confidence in it is partially dependent upon extra-Community factors. The European Court of Justice recognised in Opinion 1/76 that the Community's internal competence necessarily comports an external aspect—

> '[external power] flows by implication from the provisions of the Treaty . . . insofar as the participation of the Community in the international agreement is . . . necessary for the attainment of one of the objectives of the Community.'[109]

The Community is thus said to have external powers which run necessarily 'parallel' to its internal powers:

[107] See G Hadfield, 'Privatizing Commercial Law: Lessons from the Middle and Digital Ages' (http://papers.ssrn.com, 2000), arguing that the globalisation of commerce is stimulating the creation and application of private rules which are overseen by the state.

[108] G Betlem and E Hondius, 'European Private Law after the Treaty of Amsterdam' (2001) *European Review of Private Law* 3, at 10.

[109] Opinion 1/76 re: *The Draft Agreement for a Laying-up Fund for Inland Waterway Vessels*, [1976] ECR 741, at para 4. In that case the Court ruled that the Community had exclusive competence to sign an international agreement on traffic on the Moselle and Rhine rivers, given the fact that such an agreement had to include a third country, Switzerland. See generally, C Kotuby, 'External Competence of the European Community in the Hague Conference on private international law: Community harmonization and worldwide unification' (2001) *Netherlands International Law Review* 1.

> 'Parallelism is not only a mechanism or rationale for implied powers; it is a fundamental aspect of the nature of Community competence. It is just not possible any longer—if it ever was—for the Community to pursue its objectives solely within its own internal "space."' *Marise Cremona.*[110]

Whilst binding international regulation is inherently difficult to achieve, even non-binding agreements can have substantial impact.[111] The economic benefits of e-commerce give the international community a powerful incentive to create rules which will generate confidence in it. Even those States in which e-commerce is not a high priority might be expected to participate for fear of seeing instruments adopted without their input.[112] Further, the international community can exert significant pressures on States who might be tempted to attract business by establishing themselves as 'safe havens' from international regulation.[113] Even the US, which has traditionally adopted an insular attitude to international legal co-operation, has shown significant interest in the area recently.[114]

The following chapters, after analysing the threats to producers' and consumers' critical interests, discuss the potential of self-help, and then go on to deal with the extent to which the Community fulfils the three roles of first, supporting self-help, second, offering substantive protection, and third, facilitating the vindication of rights across borders.

[110] M Cremona, 'External relations and external competence: the emergence of an integrated policy,' in P Craig and G de Búrca (eds), *The Evolution of EU Law* (Oxford, OUP, 1999) at 147. See for example the discussion in chapter 3 of the Directive on data protection—the Directive lays down the conditions under which personal data may be transferred to third countries.

[111] See generally, D Harland, 'The Consumer in the Globalised Information Society: the Impact of the International Organisations', paper presented at the 7th International Consumer Law Conference, Helsinki, May 1999.

[112] A classic example of the type of danger involved is that of the USSR's abandonment of its seat in the UN Security Council in the 1950s, which allowed a peace-keeping force to be sent to Korea.

[113] See for example how this has happened with regard to tax law within a general context—the Fiscal Affairs Committee of the OECD in June 2000 requested that 35 countries reform their laws to negate the effects of their 'harmful' status as tax havens, the Committee threatening a powerful catalogue of sanctions if they refused (see OECD, *The OECD, Tax Competition, and the Future of Tax Reform*, http://www.oecd.org//daf/FSM/taxcompetitionarticle.html, 2000). At least one self-proclaimed 'state' has sought to attract Internet-related business by offering itself as a haven from public regulation—'Sealand'—a decommissioned naval tower 7 miles from the British coast (*Financial Times*, 6 June 2000, 4).

[114] This can be seen for example in the Safe Harbour Agreement on Privacy, discussed in chapter 3 below, in the ratification of the Berne Convention (in 1989) and of the WIPO Internet Treaties, discussed in chapter 5 below, and in the establishment of the ICANN Process, discussed in chapter 6 below. See generally, A Boss, 'Electronic Commerce and the Symbiotic Relationship Between International and Domestic Law Reform' (1998) 72 *Tulane Law Review* 1931. See also, outside the field of commercial law, the recent US signing of the Treaty establishing the International Criminal Court: www.iccnow.org.

2

Consumers I—Fair Trading Interests

Threats to Consumers' Fair Trading Interests

The borderlessness of the Net can make it easy for *fraudulent marketing* to deceive vulnerable consumers. Consumers will often not appreciate the *extent* of this borderlessness—for example, the fact that a site using a 'co.uk' domain may be based outside the UK, or that a Swedish-language 'dot.com' site is based outside Sweden. The Net's transience, size and capacity to support anonymity can further incubate fraud. A Web site can be set up in minutes with little or no requirement of verified identity.[1] It can disappear within the same time-frame. Once established, a site will generally be accessible from all over the world. This makes the online impersonation of another entity ('spoofing') relatively easy—an old man online can easily pass himself off as a young woman and vice-versa.[2] A variety of fraudulent practices common in

[1] See for example the facilities offered by www.geocities.com.

[2] On the related problem of online identity theft, see United States Federal Trade Commission, 'FTC targets identity fraud' (www.ftc.gov/opa/2000/02/idtheft.htm, 2000). The FTC details most of the problems as financial and include in particular the scarring of victims' credit rating, and victims having to prove they were not responsible for certain purchases in their name in order to avoid the attentions of debt collectors. As noted in chapter 1, the growth of online fraud is generating pressure for change to the Net's capacity to support anonymity (see

the off-line world have surfaced on the Web; the National Consumers League in the US in 2002 listed the following as the top ten frauds:

— 1 Online auctions,
— 2 General merchandise,
— 3 Nigerian money offers,
— 4 Computer equipment,
— 5 Internet access services,
— 6 Work-at-home schemes,
— 7 Information/adult services,
— 8 Travel,
— 9 Advance-fee loans,
— 10 Prizes/sweepstakes.[3]

Another common scam is the pyramid scheme, involving the collection of money in return for the granting of rights to recruit new individuals for the scheme, or their actual recruitment. Clearly, these schemes must fail as the recruiting cannot go on forever and when it ends, those at the bottom of the 'pyramid' lose their money.[4]

A good example of how the Internet's characteristics can support fraud comes from the United States Federal Trade Commission, which in 1998 uncovered a scam which lured consumers into downloading a 'viewer' in order to descramble free pornographic images; in fact the 'viewer' disconnected consumers' modems and dialled a premium-rate telephone number in Moldavia.[5]

Consumers' information interest is challenged by the ephemeral and partially-anonymous nature of the Net. In terms of seeking reliable information about a business prior to dealing with it, consumers will often not know where to look or have the time to find out. A Web site or e-mail may contain a misleading representation of the goods or services on offer, and if a problem arises post-purchase, the relevant Web-page may have changed without the consumer knowing, or, if he does know it has changed, without him having any way of proving it.

also the discussion below of the EU's Directive on e-commerce which, amongst other things, provides for information society service providers to give various details about themselves).

[3] (http://www.fraud.org/2002intstats.htm).

[4] The FTC for example has undertaken a number of cases against operators of pyramid schemes, see further *Prepared Statement of the Federal Trade Commission on 'Internet Fraud' Before the Subcommittee on Investigations of the Governmental Affairs Committee* (www.ftc.gov/os/1998/9802/internet.test.htm, 1998).

[5] FTC, *In the Matter of Baylen Telecom, Ltd. and others* (www.ftc.gov/os/1998/9802/beylen.cmp.htm, 1998). These scams have been ongoing for some time, the FTC's first case involving the Internet, concerning a credit repair scam, was filed in 1994, *FTC v Corzine*, CIV–S–94–1446 (ED Cal. filed 12 Sept. 1994) per L Rozell and R Starek, 'The Federal Trade Commission's Commitment to On-line Consumer Protection' (1997) 14 *John Marshall Journal of Computer and Information Law* 679 at 687.

Surveys have shown that these problems are real. A study conducted by Consumers International in 1999 found that 28 per cent of Web sites surveyed provided no geographical contact address, and that 40 per cent of sites surveyed did not provide contract terms.[6] Another international survey of the same year, undertaken by the Federal Trade Commission, produced similar results, finding that 16 per cent of sites failed to provide a geographic address, that 67.5 per cent of sites failed to disclose the delivery timescale, and that 47 per cent of sites did not disclose the total costs to be paid.[7]

Pre-contractual problems are mirrored post-contract, including in particular a problem which does not exist in the typical offline consumer purchase—the non-arrival of the goods. The Consumers International study noted above found that 9 per cent of goods ordered failed to arrive.[8] The survey also found quality problems extant at delivery with 8 per cent of purchases—including goods being damaged on arrival, electrical items not having the correct plugs fitted, wrongly completed orders and a case of champagne being left outside in freezing weather.[9] In such cases, the consumer may face difficulties in communicating with the seller, due to problems associated with cost, language and the absence of face-to-face contact. The return of goods will typically involve initial financial outlay by the consumer, and any requirement to return online deliveries such as software will often be technically difficult.[10]

Typical *offline payment mechanisms* such as cash and card offer some level of security through possession. In the electronic marketplace the interest in secure payment is challenged by the ease with which payment card details and related information can be misappropriated online. Such misappropriation may occur through insecure databases or through insecure lines of communication.[11] The latter problem would now appear largely historical, as modern transfers of payment information are usually securely encrypted—the problem of misappropriation of payment card details revolved around 'packet sniffer' programs which searched for packets of information containing strings of numbers in the

[6] *Consumers@shopping* (www.e-global.es/libros.html) at 37. The survey involved researchers from consumer organisations in eleven participating countries who were instructed to buy eight typical consumer products from both one domestic and one foreign site, giving a sample of 151 purchases in seventeen countries.

[7] *FTC International Web Survey: Disclosure of General Business and Contract-Related Information by Online Retailers* (www.ftc.gov/opa/1999/9906/internationalwebsurvey.htm, 1999).

[8] Note 6 above, at 37.

[9] Note 6 above, at 38.

[10] Of course the return of defective software will rarely be strictly necessary, however sellers may want online deliveries returned so that they can identify the source of the problem.

[11] These problems are not limited to consumers of course, the first electronic bank heist occurred in 1994 when the Russian Vladimir Levin extracted over $10 million from a number of Citibank corporate accounts. Although Levin was eventually caught, Citibank were unable to discover how he stole the money, nor to identify the accounts to which it was transferred, see Hill & Knowlton, *Study on Remote Banking* (Report to Directorate-General Consumer Protection of the European Commission, 1998) at 50–1.

format used on payment cards.[12] However, it would also appear that the problem of insecure databases is a current one—in the year 2000 a string of Internet security breaches were reported in the UK, including a series of thefts in August from the online bank *Egg*.[13] These issues would appear to be part of a long line of problems with payment technology dating back to the 'phantom cash withdrawal' problems of the 1980s.[14] The facility of operating at a distance clearly has attractions not just for consumers, but also for fraudsters.

Looking in the round at online consumer problems it seems clear that they are significant and growing. Whilst the Net is responsible for just 1 per cent of VISA's sales in Europe, it accounts for 47 per cent of its charge-backs.[15] This situation is mirrored in the US—the National Consumers League[16] saw the number of Net-related complaints it received multiply tenfold between 1996 and 1998.[17]

The following section considers the capacity of self-help to solve these problems.

Self-help as a Solution?

The touchstones of proponents of self-help are fair-trading marks (or 'trustmarks'), payment intermediaries and Alternative Dispute Resolution ('ADR') schemes. These mechanisms are important given the fact that consumer disputes will often not be sufficiently valuable to justify court action;[18] they will now be considered in turn.

[12] However, it has been shown to be possible for a remote fraudster to capture security information in real-time from an Internet banking customer, using a macro contained in an email message: BBC 'Crime Squad' programme of 22 November 1999.

[13] See BBC, 'Egg fraud fears grow' (http://news6.thdo.bbc.co.uk/hi/english/business/newsid per cent5F894000/894994.stm). The problem of security breaches via the Web has also in the UK in 2000 affected Barclays Bank, Abbey National and Powergen.

[14] See Hill & Knowlton, note 11 above, at 51. Those problems revolved around bank employees illicitly retrieving customers' Personal Identification Numbers.

[15] J MacGowan, 'E-commerce from a retailer's perspective', paper delivered at the Conference on E-commerce, University of Sheffield, 16 July 1999, at 1. See also, R Brownsword and J MacGowan, 'Credit Card Fraud' (1997) 147 *New Law Journal* 1806. (However, *VISA* claims that overall fraudulent use of its cards is in decline—0.18% of total transaction volume in 1992, down to 0.06% in 1999: VISA press release, 'VISA USA fraud levels reach all-time low' (www.visa.com/av/news/main.ghtml, 24 February 2000).)

[16] An independent, non-profit body. The League has a program of monitoring fraud on the Net—*Internet Fraud Watch*, www.fraud.org/internet/intstat.htm, see also: www.nclnet.org/internetscamfactsheet.html.

[17] At www.fraud.org/internet/intset.htm.

[18] In 1998 it was estimated that a cross-border claim in the EU (under the Brussels Convention 1968—now superseded by a Regulation, discussed below at p 49) was only worth pursuing if in excess of 2000 euros: European Consumer Law Group, *Jurisdiction and Applicable Law in Cross-border Consumer Complaints* (http://europa.eu.int/comm/consumers/policy/eclg/reports_en.html, 1998) at 3.

Fair-trading marks can offer consumers reassurance about the general legitimacy of a trader. A number of marks have been established by business and by consumer organisations; a typical example of the latter was the *Which? Web Trader* scheme of the UK Consumers' Association, which ran from 1999 to 2002.[19] This scheme provided online certification (logo and code of conduct) in the UK, and, in co-operation with consumer organisations abroad, in six other EU Member States. It guaranteed levels of consumer care in relation to:

> 1) contract terms, 2) price information, 3) delivery terms, 4) security, 5) advertising, 6) consumer law generally,[20] 7) promotions, 8) identity and location of the seller, 9) refunds, 10) guarantees, 11) receipts, 12) co-operation with *Which? Legal Service* in the event of dispute, 13) complaint handling and dispute resolution, 14) data protection, 15) customer support, 16) service and feedback.

The very involvement of consumer organisations in sponsoring sites has the capacity to generate consumer confidence in the sites for obvious reasons, and in some systems the mark may be capable of becoming part of the contract between the consumer and the trader. The *Which? Web Trader* mark, had been taken up by 1603 sites as of May 2001.[21] The temporary success of the mark would indicate that it served to generate a significant amount of confidence—it is not clear why it folded.

An example of a fair-trading mark established by a business organisation is the *Internet Shopping is Safe* logo of the Interactive Media in Retail Group in the UK.[22] The logo can be clicked to verify, and promises that registered sites:

— have undertaken to trade in a manner that is legal, decent, honest, truthful and fair;
— have had their sites and service reviewed by IMRG;
— will be monitored by IMRG;
— had their Business, VAT and Data Protection registrations checked by IMRG.

Despite their benefits, fair-trading marks are not a panacea to the problems outlined above. Marks cannot *compel* traders to uphold their standards of consumer care, but can only threaten them with the general sanction of withdrawing the mark if they do not. This provides no relief to the individual consumer who has suffered detriment.

Nor are fair-trading marks of use where they are not recognised. Only a small fraction of the world's consumers would currently recognise any given trustmark. Whilst the electronic marketplace is global, the consumer is 'local' in respect of trusting consumer associations. The consumer associations which

[19] See http://www.which.net/webtrader. The reasons for its closure are not clear. The Consumers' Association was never before involved in ongoing certification of traders (although it has traditionally carried out periodic, independent testing).

[20] This is not further defined.

[21] http://whichwebtrader.which.net/webtrader/index.html.

[22] www.imrg.org.

lie behind trustmarks are inherently national (although they may co-ordinate their efforts, as in the case of *Which? Web Trader* above). Finally, and perhaps most importantly, most e-commerce sites do not currently carry any mark.

A further self-help mechanism is consumer use of a known and trusted payment intermediary, such as a credit card company, which can help to reassure consumers about the integrity of an online trader. Certain credit cards enjoy high levels of recognition amongst consumers across the world,[23] and given that card companies generally settle traders' accounts in arrears, if problems arise with goods or services the company can easily stop payment; a trader who generates a disproportionate number of complaints can expect to have its authorisation to take payment withdrawn.

Despite these positive points, payment intermediaries do not solve all of consumers' online problems. They are not used by all sites, nor are they held by, or available to, all consumers.[24] No intermediary is present in e-cash[25] transactions, which although not currently common, may become so as technology develops. Where payment intermediaries are used, their interests do not always coincide with those of individual consumers. Intermediaries' interests centre around the general legitimacy of traders, rather than around the protection of consumers' interests per se. Accepting a consumer dispute as legitimate may result in financial loss to the intermediary, in particular if it has already paid the trader in question. Evidence of intermediaries' reluctance to guarantee individual transactions can be found in the United Kingdom, where credit card companies have consistently refused to accept that their general statutory liability as connected lenders applies to international sales.[26] Another example of how financial institutions are prone to pursue their own interests at the expense of those of individual consumers comes from the phantom cash withdrawal cases of the 1980s—one study of these cases concluded that, despite undeniable knowledge of in-house ATM fraud, 'many [UK] banks had a deliberate policy of denying that sophisticated ATM fraud was possible.'[27]

[23] For example *VISA*, accepted at over 21 million locations around the world: www.visa.com/av/who/main.html.

[24] For example, it has been estimated that only 50% of Britain's adult population has use of a credit card: National Consumer Council, *E-commerce and consumer protection* (http://www.ncc.org.uk/pubs/pdf/ecommerce.pdf., 2000) at 7.

[25] See eg www.mondex.com.

[26] The question arises as the relevant statutory provision—section 75 of the Consumer Credit Act 1974—does not specify whether it applies to international sales. Although credit card companies do not accept an *obligation* to guarantee international transactions, some do so voluntarily, see OECD, *Consumer Redress in the Global Marketplace: Chargebacks* (www.oecd.org/dsti/sti/it/consumer/prod/e_96-142.htm, 1996) at 21.

[27] The problem was clearly known to the banks because they had supported criminal prosecutions of employees who had made 'phantom withdrawals' from ATM machines: Hill & Knowlton, note 11 above, at 51 (the Report details similar problems in Germany). See generally, R Anderson, 'Why Cryptosystems Fail' (http://www.cl.cam.ac.uk/Research/Security/studies/st-rs.html, 1994).

As regards self-help in the field of post-purchase disputes, ADR can offer solutions, as has been emphasised by both the private and the public sector. Regarding the private sector, the Global Business Dialogue on E-commerce has established a working group on the matter:

> 'GBDe will commence a new initiative through its members to foster the development of consumer protection and alternative dispute resolution mechanisms designed to promote fair business practices across international borders. These mechanisms will be designed to permit consumers, wherever they are located, to enjoy basic protections against false and misleading advertising and marketing practices, and to have access to private redress for violations of those protections.'[28]

As regards the public sector, the OECD Guidelines on Consumer Protection in Electronic Commerce 1999 state:

> 'businesses, consumer representatives and governments should work together to continue to use and develop fair, effective and transparent self-regulatory and other policies and procedures, including alternative dispute resolution mechanisms, to address consumer complaints and to resolve consumer disputes arising from business-to-consumer electronic commerce, with special attention to cross-border transactions.'[29]

ADR has proved successful in the field of commercial disputes,[30] and it has many positive aspects in relation to consumer e-commerce—it offers rapid, low-cost, online dispute resolution which avoids the technicalities of legal rules. There is evidence to suggest that cross-border consumer ADR can work as long as both parties agree to it,[31] and various online schemes are in operation.[32] However, notwithstanding these positive aspects, ADR suffers the same major drawback as payment intermediaries and fair trading marks, that of non-universality. Consumers cannot rely on the fact that sellers will submit to ADR schemes, and even if they can, the initial financial outlay required of consumers will discourage many of them, particularly in relation to small-scale purchases.[33]

To conclude, self-help has the capacity to offer only limited protection to consumers' fair trading interest—trading marks and payment intermediaries

[28] http://www.gbd.org/structure/working/adr.html.

[29] www.oecd.org/subject/e_commerce/ at VI(B). See also the relevant provisions of the Directive on e-commerce, discussed below.

[30] See in particular the growth in use of arbitration: T Carbonneau (ed), *Lex Mercatoria and arbitration : a discussion of the new law merchant* (Boston, Kluwer Law International, 1998).

[31] See C Last and J Nijgh, 'The Dutch system of alternative dispute resolution schemes relating to consumer disputes in the European Union' (1999) 7(4) *Consumer Law Journal* 417 at 440.

[32] See eg cybersettle.com and clicknsettle.com which offer mediation services. See generally, J Hornle, 'Disputes Solved in Cyberspace and the Rule of Law' 2001(2) *Journal of International Law and Technology* (http://elj.warwick.ac.uk/jilt/01-2/hornle.html).

[33] See generally, M Cappelletti, 'Alternative Dispute Resolution Processes within the Framework of the World-Wide Access-to-Justice Movement' (1993) 56 *Modern Law Review* 282.

can act as familiar touchstones for consumers buying at a distance and exert general quality controls on sellers; ADR can sometimes bring rapid resolution of post-contractual problems. However, consumers thinking about buying online have no *guarantee* that these mechanisms will protect their interests, and this leaves a gap for public regulation to fill. The following section investigates how far the European Community does so.

Community Regulation

> 'In order to realize the commercial and cultural potential of the Internet, consumers must have confidence that the goods and services offered are fairly represented, that they will get what they pay for, and that recourse or redress will be available if they do not. This is an area where government action is appropriate . . .'
> *US President Clinton and Vice-President Gore.*[34]

The Community has for some time recognised the need for public action to solve the problems outlined above. The Community's actions will be dealt with in terms of support for self-help, substantive protection and finally cross-border co-ordination.

Support for Self-help

The Community's support for self-help is concentrated in the fields of codes of conduct and ADR systems. The Directive on e-commerce[35] makes provision for the development of codes of conduct to ensure that commercial parties comply autonomously with identified information duties imposed on them by the Directive (these duties are discussed in the section '*Substantive protection*' below):

> '1. Member States and the Commission shall encourage:
> (a) the drawing up of codes of conduct at Community level, by trade, professional and consumer associations or organisations, designed to contribute to the proper implementation of Articles 5 to 15;[36]

[34] *A Framework for Electronic Commerce,* (www.whitehouse.gov/eleccomm.htm, 1997) at 27. See also the comments of the Australian Department of Industry: 'The successful enforcement of laws relating to trading practices and fraud is crucial to establishing a favourable environment in which consumers can do business', *Untangling the Web: Electronic Commerce and the Consumer* (http://www.dist.gov.au/consumer/publicat/untangle/index.html, 1999) at 24.

[35] Directive 2000/31/EC on certain legal aspects of information society services, in particular electronic commerce, in the Internal Market, OJ 2000 L178/1. See also, Commission, *Proposal for a European Parliament and Council Directive on certain legal aspects of electronic commerce in the internal market,* COM(98) 586.

[36] Relating to informational duties, commercial communications, contracts concluded by electronic means, and the liability of intermediary service providers.

> (b) the voluntary transmission of draft codes of conduct at national or Community level to the Commission;
> (c) the accessibility of these codes of conduct in the Community languages by electronic means;
> (d) the communication to the Member States and the Commission, by trade, professional and consumer associations or organisations, of their assessment of the application of their codes of conduct and their impact upon practices, habits or customs relating to electronic commerce . . .;
> 2. Member States and the Commission shall encourage the involvement of associations or organisations representing consumers in the drafting and implementation of codes of conduct affecting their interests and drawn upon accordance with paragraph 1(a). Where appropriate, to take account of their specific needs, associations representing the visually impaired and disabled should be consulted.' (Article 16).

The Directive on distance contracts makes similar provision.[37] Further, in 2001 the Commission adopted a Recommendation on the principles applicable to the bodies responsible for out-of-court settlement of consumer disputes.[38] The Recommendation lays down non-binding standards for settlement bodies in relation to impartiality, fair trading, effectiveness and fairness.

The Directive on e-commerce also gives support to out-of-court dispute settlement.

> '1. Member States shall ensure that, in the event of disagreement between an information society service provider and the recipient of the service, their legislation does not hamper the use of out-of-court schemes, available under national law, for dispute settlement, including appropriate electronic means.
> 2. Member States shall encourage bodies responsible for the out-of-court dispute settlement of, in particular, consumer disputes to operate in a way which provides adequate procedural guarantees for the parties concerned.' (Article 17).

The above provisions for out-of-court settlement were bolstered by the establishment in 2001 of a European Extra-Judicial Network for the resolution of consumer disputes.[39] The Network covers all the Member States as well as Norway and Iceland, and links a series of contact points or 'Clearing Houses' (eg the Association of British Travel Agents in the UK) which provide consumers with information on available ADR schemes, as well as legal advice and practical help in pursuing a complaint by this means. Via the Network's

[37] Directive 97/7/EC on the protection of consumers in respect of distance contracts: 'Member States may provide that voluntary supervision of compliance with the provisions of this Directive entrusted to self-regulatory bodies and recourse to such bodies to settle disputes are added to the means which Member States must provide to ensure compliance with the provisions of this Directive.' (Article 11(4)).

[38] Recommendation 2001/310/EC, see also earlier Recommendation 98/257/EC: http://www.europa.eu.int/comm/consumers/redress/out_of_court/adr/index_en.htm.

[39] Decision 2001/470. See http://www.eejnet.org/.

Web-site consumers can access a unified complaint form in thirteen languages. Furthermore, the Commission is considering the case for a European Consumer Ombudsman with competence for cross-border complaints.[40]

Substantive Protection

The Community has adopted two instruments of particular relevance to consumer confidence in e-commerce, the Directives on e-commerce[41] and on distance contracts.[42] The adoption of these Directives in 2000 and 1997 respectively can be viewed as positive given the slow pace at which the Community legislature often moves; the Directive on distance contracts can be seen as particularly perspicacious, stemming from a 1992 Proposal[43] which was ahead of its time in recognising the challenges presented by emerging communications technology.[44] However, the final product did not live up to early promise, as seems often to be the case with Community Directives on consumer law.[45]

[40] Report on consumer complaints in respect of distance selling and comparative advertising, COM(2000) 127.

[41] Note 35 above. The Directive is not restricted to the consumer field, but establishes generally-applicable rules governing information society services (including in particular businesses selling over the Net). 'Information society services' are defined by the Directive as including, 'any service normally provided for remuneration, at a distance, by electronic means and at the individual request of a recipient of services' (Article 2(a)). The rights granted to consumers under national law transposing the Directive cannot be waived by the consumer, nor can those rights be excluded by the choice of law of a non-Member State where the contract has a close connection with the territory of one or more Member States (Article 12).

[42] Note 37 above.

[43] Commission, *Proposal for a Council Directive on the protection of consumers in respect of contracts negotiated at a distance*, OJ 1992 C156/14, amended at OJ 1993 C308/18 ('Proposal').

[44] See, for example, Recital 3 which reads: 'Whereas the development of new technologies is multiplying the means available to consumers to have knowledge of offers being made everywhere in the Community and the placing orders . . .' Further, the Explanatory Memorandum accompanying the Proposal makes reference to the Fourth Community Action Plan for Consumer Policy (1990–92) (COM(90)98), which stated that, 'cross-frontier selling by electronic means using television and new communications technology, in addition to existing mail-order business, will stimulate demand for cross-frontier purchasing,' at 1. It should be noted that the Internet is not mentioned in the Proposal, unsurprising in view of the fact that the Internet was then in its commercial infancy (commercial activity was only permitted on the Internet from 1991). As the title of the Proposal indicates, it concerned contracts made at a distance generally, rather than just contracts made on the Internet.

[45] For example Directive 99/44/EC on guarantees, significantly narrower than the original Green Paper of 1993 (Commission, *Green Paper on Guarantees for Consumer Goods and After-Sales Services*, COM(93) 509. See generally: H Beale and G Howells, 'EC Harmonisation of Consumer Sales Law—A missed opportunity?' (1997) 12 *Journal of Contract Law* 21; R Bradgate and C Twigg-Flesner, 'The EC Directive On Certain Aspects of the Sale of Consumer Goods and Associated Guarantees—All Talk and No Do?' [2000] 2 *Web Journal of Current Legal Issues* (http://webjcli.ncl.ac.uk/2000/contents2.html).

Both the Directive on e-commerce and the Directive on distance contracts contain serious flaws in the protection they offer to consumers' interests (although it should be noted that the Directive on distance contracts is of minimum character).[46]

First, the Directive on distance contracts adopts a restrictive definition of 'distance contract'. It would seem that whenever consumers agree to buy something at a distance they are exposed to the problems of buying 'in the dark', and should thus benefit from the protection offered by the Directive. Unfortunately, the Directive is not all-encompassing in this regard. Its definition of 'distance contract' revolves around the *exclusive use* of distance communication:

> '"distance contract" means any contract concerning goods or services concluded between a supplier and a consumer under a distance sales or service-provision scheme run by the supplier, who, for the purpose of the contract, makes exclusive use of one or more means of distance communication up to and including the moment at which the contract is concluded.' (Article 2(1)).

Thus the Directive would not appear to cover the situation where a supplier demonstrates a product to a consumer in person, but sells it via distance communication (unless such a situation could be included by arguing that the supplier has exclusively used distance communication *for the purposes of the contract*, the fact that the supplier has had face-to-face contact with the consumer *for the purposes of selling* being incidental).

Second, the Directive on distance contracts excludes from its scope contracts for financial services (including insurance, banking, pension and investment services).[47] The reason for this exclusion was evidently the intention to bring forward sector-specific regulation, now embodied in Directive 2002/65 on the distance marketing of consumer financial services.[48] Yet it is difficult to see why financial services could not have been included within the scope of the original Directive; of course, a financial service cannot be returned in the same way as a T-shirt, but this is true of services generally, which are included in the Directive. Furthermore, the rationale for protecting consumers who buy at a distance—that they are buying 'in the dark'—applies to contracts for financial services as much as to any other contract. Indeed it can be argued that consumers are especially in need of protection in this area, as financial services are unusual in their complexity and expense, and consumers are often inexpe-

[46] Article 14: 'Member States may maintain or introduce more stringent provisions than those contained in the Directive in order to ensure a higher level of consumer protection.' The Directive on e-commerce is of maximum character within its co-ordinated field, which is defined in note 51 below.

[47] Article 3(1).

[48] OJ (2002) L271/16.

rienced in dealing with them. Certainly, the financial services industry is by no means immune from creating consumer problems, as demonstrated for example by recent mis-selling of pensions and endowment-mortgages in the UK, and by the periodic collapse of banks. The real explanation for the exclusion of financial services contracts from the Directive would seem to lie, as with other Community and national instruments, in the lobbying power of the financial services industry.[49]

The extent to which the instruments above protect consumers' interest in fair marketing practices will now be discussed.

Fair Marketing Practices

The Directive on e-commerce applies the principle of home country control[50] to regulation of online marketing within the Community:

> 'Member States may not, for reasons falling within this Directive's coordinated field[[51]] restrict the freedom to provide Information Society services[[52]] from another Member State.' Article 3(2).[53]

This principle is beneficial to sellers, who have to comply with only one Member States' marketing laws. However, it does not reflect the national variations in consumers' conceptions of 'fairness' in relation to marketing practices. The Preamble to the Directive maintains that,

> 'The Court of Justice has consistently held that a Member State retains the right to take measures against a service provider that is established in another Member State but directs all or most of his activity to the territory of the first Member State in question if the choice of establishment was made with a view to evading the

[49] See for example the special provision made for insurance contracts within the Directive 13/93/EC on unfair terms in consumer contracts, and within the United Kingdom's Unfair Contract Terms Act 1977 (Schedule 1(1)(a)).

[50] In line with Articles 28 and 49 of the Treaty (see Case C–384/93 *Alpine Investments BV v Minister van Financien* [1995] ECR I–1141. See generally N Dethloff, 'European conflict-of-law provisions governing unfair competition' (April 2000) 32 *Commercial Communications* 14, who notes that the Directive has been part of a drive to review unfair competition law in Germany, due to fears that its strict laws may place it a competitive disadvantage.

[51] The 'co-ordinated field' is defined as: 'requirements laid down in Member States' legal systems applicable to information society service providers or information society services, regardless of whether they are of a general nature or specifically designed for them . . .' (Article 2 (h)).

[52] Note 46 above.

[53] Article 3(2) is subject to a number of exceptions and to derogation in exceptional cases: Article 3(4) and Annex. Exceptional measures must be necessary, proportionate and taken against a given information society service provider (Article 3(4)). Member States can restrict the freedom to provide an Information Society service as long as: the 'home' Member State is first asked to take measures and fails adequately to do so and the Commission is notified (Article 3(4)(b)). In urgent cases, these provisions can be applied after action is taken (Article 3(5)).

legislation that would have applied to the provider if he had been established on the territory of the first Member State.' (Recital 57).[54]

Notwithstanding Recital 57, the Directive does not deal with the situation of a service-provider who directs only a *minority* of his activity to the territory of a particular Member State. The service provider may sell to very large numbers of consumers in a given Member State, without those sales constituting 'all or most of his activity'. Further, it will often not be possible to prove that a choice of establishment was made to evade a particular Member States' legislation. A service-provider may be able to argue plausibly yet falsely that a choice was made for tax-, technical- or labour-related reasons. Home country control imposes geographical, political, cultural and linguistic distances between regulators and the individuals affected by the regulation which is greater than that which would exist if the 'targeted'[55] country was the controller.[56] The 'home country' regulator might be expected to experience external resource constraints which dictate that a low priority is given to the problems of foreign consumers. The impact of home country control has been seen in the area of satellite television, where television channels directed entirely at one country (as is clear by virtue of the language used) are regulated in another country simply because it is in the latter they are uploaded to a satellite.[57]

In 2003 the Commission attempted to bolster the Directive on e-commerce with its Proposal for a Directive on Unfair Commercial Practices.[58] The Proposal suggests the establishment of a uniform Community prohibition of unfair business-to-consumer practices harming consumers' economic interests; it will not be dealt with further here, as its future is uncertain—although the Competitiveness Council reached political agreement on the Proposal on

[54] Recital 57. See also the definition of 'established service provider': 'a service provider who effectively pursues an economic activity using a fixed establishment for an indefinite period. The presence and use of the technical means and technologies required to provide the service do not, in themselves, constitute an establishment of the provider.' (Article 2(c)).

[55] By 'targeting' is meant the directing of activities as discussed in relation to the Brussels Regulation at 49 below.

[56] Compare Dethloff, note 50 above, who does not envisage problems with the home country control principle, arguing in particular that the competitive advantage to be gained from *relocation* is minimal, at 23.

[57] See: Directive 89/522/EEC ('Television Without Frontiers Directive'), OJ 1989 L298/23, as amended by Directive 978/36/EC, OJ 1997 L202; also Case C–34–36/95 *Konsumentenombudsmannen (KO) v De Agostini (Svenska) Forlag AB and TV-Shop i Sverige AB* [1998] 1 CMLR 32, in which the Court ruled that the Directive precluded the application to television broadcasts from other Member States of a provision of a domestic broadcasting law providing that advertisements broadcast in commercial breaks on television must not be designed to attract the attention of children under 12 years of age (whilst leaving Sweden some room for maneouvre in acting against advertisers in other non-discriminatory and proportionate ways). The home country control principle is also applied by the EU in the fields of insurance and banking.

[58] COM(2003) 356.

the 18th May 2004,[59] a second reading is due to take place in the European Parliament in autumn 2004 and it is not clear what the outcome of that reading will be.[60]

Information Interests

> 'Whereas the use of means of distance communication must not lead to a reduction in the information provided to the consumer.' *Recital 11, Directive 97/7/EC on distance contracts.*

The Directive on e-commerce mandates online businesses to give certain information about themselves and their products, including: the company's name, geographic and electronic address;[61] and clear price information.[62] Further, certain information must be given to consumers prior to an order being placed, including the technical steps necessary to conclude the contract, a copy of the contract in such a way that allows the consumer to store and reproduce it, whether or not the contract will be filed by the business, and whether it will be accessible.[63]

In addition to the Directive on e-commerce, the Directive on distance contracts requires the seller to inform the consumer of, amongst other things, the identity of the supplier, the main characteristics and inclusive price of the goods, and the consumer's right of withdrawal.[64] This information is required to be provided 'in good time prior to the conclusion of the contract',[65] and, 'with due regard . . . to the principles of good faith in commercial transactions . . .' (Article 4(2)). The incorporation of the principles of good faith is supportive of consumers' interests as it can be argued that it enables the Directive to respond to changing circumstances and to take account of the particular characteristics of individual consumer-seller relationships.[66]

[59] Council Document 9667/04. Sweden and Denmark did not join the agreement.

[60] The progress of the Proposal, together with all relevant documents, can be followed at http://europa.eu.int/comm/consumers/index_en.htm. See also: G Howells, 'Proposed Directive on Unfair Commercial Practices' (2003), www.iacl.ca/researchpapers.

[61] Article 5.

[62] *Ibid.*

[63] Article 10.

[64] Article 4, discussed below.

[65] Article 4(1). This which would seem to mean that the consumer must have had time to consider the information before the conclusion of any contract, ie the seller must not seek to avoid the provision by sending the information before the conclusion of the contract in such a way that it does not reach the consumer until afterwards (eg by surface mail).

[66] See generally on the varying interpretations of 'good faith': R Zimmermann and S Whittaker (eds), *Good Faith in European Contract Law* (Cambridge University Press, 2000); M Hesselink, 'Good faith', in A Hartkamp and others (eds), *Towards a European Civil Code* (Nijmegen, Kluwer Law International, 1998), p 285; J Beatson and D Friedmann (eds), *Good Faith and Fault in Contract Law* (Oxford, Clarendon Press, 1995).

However, the Directive's scheme for the provision of prior information is flawed by the absence of specified sanctions for breach. This stands in contrast to the provisions on confirmation of details *post*-contract, where failure to comply extends the period in which the consumer can withdraw.[67] The lack of any sanction against sellers for failure to provide prior information is especially serious in view of the fact that not all mandatory prior information must be confirmed post-contract, in particular information regarding the cost of using the means of distance communication, where other than the basic rate, and any minimum duration of the contract. Although the Directive provides that Member States can choose to place the burden of proving the supply of prior information on the supplier,[68] it is difficult to envisage circumstances in which it would be reasonable to place such a burden on the consumer. In failing to provide explicitly that the seller is to bear the burden of proof, the Directive may, in line with tradition, be deferring to Member States' procedural laws,[69] but in the final analysis it fails to guarantee consumers' interests.

As stated above, information provided to the consumer before the conclusion of a contract over the Net will often be in a form which is prima facie non-durable, such as a Web page. Thus it is important that after the conclusion of the contract, consumers receive a copy of it in a durable form. The Directive does protect this interest:

> 'The consumer must receive written confirmation or confirmation in another durable medium available and accessible to him of the information referred to in Article 4(1)(a) to (f),[[70]] in good time during the performance of the contract, and at the latest at the time of delivery . . .' (Article 5).

It is positive that Article 5 makes reference to the individual circumstances of the consumer—confirmation in a medium available and accessible 'to him'—thus a seller would be in breach if a consumer without a video player were sent information on a video cassette, or a consumer without access to the Internet were to have an e-mail account set up for her and the information sent there. However it is not clear whether 'durable medium' means a medium durable of itself (eg paper), or if it is sufficient for a medium to be durable on further action by the consumer (eg a Web-page or e-mail which can be saved or printed by the consumer). The Directive provides for cancellation notices to be given 'in writing', which would indicate that the latter interpretation is correct. However, consumer confidence would have benefited from the Directive using

[67] Article 6.

[68] Article 11(3)(a).

[69] See generally, M Hoskins, 'Tilting the Balance: Supremacy and National Procedural Rules' (1996) 21 *European Law Review* 365.

[70] Supplier identity, main characteristics of the goods or services, price, delivery costs if any, arrangements for performance, the existence of the right of withdrawal.

the former interpretation, at least in the case of goods where physical delivery must occur in any event. (In the case of contracts for services it is questionable whether consumers would be willing to release geographical (or electronic) contact details, and assuming that 'receipt' can occur on the Internet, the duty could be satisfied by the provision of information electronically.) The Community has not entirely clarified its use of the same term in the Directive on the distance marketing of financial services:

> Article 2(f): 'any instrument which enables the consumer to store information addressed personally to him in a way accessible for future reference for a period of time adequate for the purposes of the information and which allows the unchanged reproduction of the information stored.'[71]

The sanction specified for failure to provide confirmation of details is an extension of the cooling-off period from seven days to three months.[72] It is not clear why the cooling-off period should expire as soon as three months when the seller is in breach of its duty to send post-contract information, particularly as the breach may result in the consumer being unaware of her right of withdrawal.[73] Extending the cooling-off period to two years, as the period of guarantee generally provided by Directive 99/44, might create the risk of heavily-used goods being returned to the seller, but such risk is generated by the seller's default.

The Directive further protects consumers' information interests by providing the right to a cooling-off period—thus consumers can check that goods and services supplied correspond with information given about them. As early as 1992, all national systems in the Community had gone some way towards recognising the importance of a right of withdrawal in distance contracts; at that time, the right could be found in relation to mail order sales in the law of seven Member States and was protected on a voluntary basis in the other five.[74]

[71] Directive 2002/65. See also Recital 20 of the Directive on distance contracts: 'durable mediums include in particular floppy discs, CD-ROMs, DVDs and the hard drive of the consumer's computer on which the electronic mail is stored, but they do not include Internet websites unless they fulfil the criteria contained in the definition of a durable medium'. The examples given in the Recital, together with the juxtaposition of 'another durable medium' with 'paper' in Article 7, imply that the medium must be inherently durable. Thus the reference to websites in the Recital must be taken to mean websites where the seller or supplier lodges the information in such a way as to be accessible by the consumer at later dates. However, an argument against this interpretation is that it is not conducive to consumer confidence for information provided for the consumer's benefit is 'stored' by the supplier, as the consumer may reasonably fear interference.

[72] Article 6.

[73] Although other Directives have not been so specific, for example, the Directive on Doorstep Contracts left to national law the matter of sanctioning failure to inform of the right of withdrawal (Council Directive 85/577/EEC on contracts negotiated away from business premises, OJ 1985 L372/31).

[74] Proposal, at Annex 1 Table 3.

The Directive provides for a cooling-off period of seven days; in the case of goods, the seven-day period runs from receipt; in the case of services, it runs from the conclusion of the contract or, if later, from the receipt by the consumer of the confirmatory details (Article 6). Whilst positive in itself, it does not apply in respect of contracts:

> '... for the supply of goods or services the price of which is dependent on fluctuations in the financial market which cannot be controlled by the supplier ...' (Article 6(3)).

Whilst it can be argued that prices are not dependent on fluctuations in the financial markets if sellers can insure against such fluctuations, this exception is so widely drawn that it risks confusing consumers as to whether they have a right of withdrawal in contracts for the many goods and services which suffer from price fluctuations in financial markets.

Further, although the consumer must be informed of her right of withdrawal (Article 5(1)), there is no stipulation that this information should be presented in a conspicuous manner, as there is in some national cooling-off provisions.[75] Article 4(2) does provide that the information must be provided in a 'clear and comprehensible manner', but this is distinct from conspicuousness. The right of withdrawal is perhaps the most important provision of the Directive. Its value is seriously diminished in cases where the consumer is not aware of her rights because the relevant information is contained in the small print of a contract, a particular problem in the case of Web contracts, where the terms are often not just in small print but separate from the principal page (ie an icon must be 'clicked' to reach the terms). Of course it might be argued that a harmonising measure such as the Directive on distance contracts is only designed to lay down the substance of the consumer's rights and it is for national law to determine matters of form. However, this would be to ignore the inter-relation of form and substance. In any event, the Directive could have referred to the importance of the consumer being made aware of the right of withdrawal.

A right of withdrawal means little to a consumer who has paid the purchase price and subsequently finds it difficult to have this money returned, and unfortunately the Directive does not make provision for the protection of advance payments. This can be a particular problem where sellers become insolvent. There are a number of examples of successful schemes for the protection of advance payments in the EU, for example that of the Association

[75] For example, the Consumer Credit Act 1974 in the UK (s61). Research has shown that consumer-understanding of disclosure information in television advertisements at least is increased by conspicuous presentation of that information: A Manrai, L Manrai and N Murray, 'Public Policy Relating to Consumer Comprehension of Television Commercials: A Review and Some Empirical Results', (1993) 16 *Journal of Consumer Policy* 145.

of British Travel Agents[76] in the UK. In Portugal, consumers cannot be required to make any payment in advance, whilst in the Netherlands it is illegal for sellers to demand more than 50 per cent of the purchase price in advance.[77] The Directive could have followed the example of those countries, or it could have made provision for the separate holding of advance payments until the expiry of the cooling-off period, or it could have established some sort of guarantee fund.

In response to the problem of late and non-existent deliveries, the Directive provides only a default rule that the supplier execute the contract within 30 days of the order.[78] This provision might be regarded as not useful at all in view of the fact that it is not mandatory.

As regards applicable law, the Directive does not specify that the choice of law must be that of the Member State which has the closest connection with the contract, only that the choice of law must be that of a Member State (Article 2(2)). Thus, it would seem from the face of the Directive that a US seller could specify French law as applicable to its contracts with UK consumers and English law as applicable to its contracts with French consumers, however Article 5(2) of the Rome Convention on the law applicable to consumer contracts (1980) prevents this, as is discussed in the section on 'co-ordination' below.

The enforcement provisions of the Directive do not reflect the diffuse nature of the consumer interest. In the event of breach of the rights given by the Directive, the value of the goods or service in question will often not justify legal action. Some provision for punitive damages for wilful breach of (at least) the Directive's provisions relating to unsolicited communications would have been useful in ensuring that those provisions are respected[79] (although the omission might be attributed to the principle of national procedural autonomy as referred to above).[80]

Furthermore, in contrast to the Directive on unfair terms,[81] Article 7 of which created a direct enforcement role for both public and private consumer organisations,[82] the Directive on distance contracts gives Member States the

[76] www.abta.co.uk. See also the Mail Order Protection Scheme (www.mops.org.uk). Both these schemes are based on a guarantee fund.

[77] Proposal, at 9.

[78] Article 7(1).

[79] Howells, note 60 above, at 9, noting that even the possibility of punitive damages would be no deterrent to rogue traders.

[80] Page 40 above.

[81] Directive 93/13, OJ 1993 L95/29.

[82] The point was raised in Case C–82/96, *R v Secretary of State for Trade and Industry ex parte No. 1 the Consumers' Association and No. 2 Which? Ltd.* (OJ 1996 C145/3), in which the defendants maintained Article 7 created no such role, although the case was withdrawn prior to judgement after the defendants capitulated. See generally, J Dickie, 'Article 7 of the Unfair Terms in Consumer Contracts Directive' [1996] *Consumer Law Journal* 112.

choice as to which public, private or professional body or bodies should have powers to police compliance with the Directive:

> '1. Member States shall ensure that adequate and effective means exist to ensure compliance with this Directive in the interests of consumers.
> 2. The means referred to in paragraph 1 shall include provisions whereby one or more of the following bodies, as determined by national law, may take action under national law before the courts or before the competent administrative bodies to ensure that the national provisions for the implementation of this Directive are applied:
> (a) public bodies or their representatives,
> (b) consumer organisations having a legitimate interest in protecting consumers,
> (c) professional organizations having a legitimate interest in acting.' (Article 11).[83]

The consumer interest would have benefited from the creation of a direct enforcement role for private consumer organisations (as envisaged in the original Proposal of 1992).[84] The value of involving private consumer organisations stems from a number of sources. Powers held by public bodies are frequently 'checked' to minimise the possibility of arbitrary action, and this makes for slow procedures. Rapid action is particularly important in the field of distance selling, where technology allows large-scale frauds to be carried out quickly and without any kind of audit trail. Government organisations are prone to 'capture' by the businesses with which they repeatedly negotiate—the relationship can become too comfortable.[85] Private consumer groups are arguably more responsive to consumer concerns than public bodies and will sometimes be the first port of call for dissatisfied consumers. The funding of public bodies can be precarious, and their effectiveness dependent on the political views of the government of the day. Consumers may be reluctant to go to a government body with their problem if they feel politically distant from the government of the day, or if it is the government itself against whom they have a complaint.

In sum, it would have been beneficial for the Directive to have laid down an enforcement standard which included enforcement powers for all organisations, private or public, domestic or foreign, with a legitimate interest in protecting consumers. There seems to be no rationale supporting the current limits of the relevant provisions. The Directive goes some way towards regulating remedies, and there seems no logical reason why it should have stopped

[83] Although it can be noted that the Directive on distance contracts is one of the instruments under which Directive 98/27 on cross-border injunctions enables 'qualified entities' to act across Member States' borders for breach and to bring actions for injunctions against those breaching Community consumer law in order to protect the collective interests of consumers.

[84] Article 13.

[85] See generally M Bernstein, *Regulating Business by Independent Commission* (Princeton University Press, 1955).

where it did. Of course, judicial review may be available to a consumer group dissatisfied with the performance of a public body, but this is too indirect a remedy to constitute effective consumer redress.

From the point of view of the individual being able to rely directly on the Directive, it is of concern that Article 12 provides, 'the consumer may not waive rights conferred on him by the transposition of this directive into national law'. Previous Directives on consumer law have spoken of the consumer not being able to waive the protection conferred by the Directive itself, rather than corresponding national law. This change in wording is most likely a rationalisation of language, doing no more than expressing the fact that consumers typically rely on transposing national laws rather than Directives themselves. However, there are situations where consumers can rely directly on Directives,[86] and the current wording of Article 12 has the potential to confuse consumers.[87]

Finally, it can be noted that the Directive granted Member States an excessively long implementation period—three years (Article 15(1)). It would seem that in order to maximise consumer confidence, this period should have been as short as reasonably practicable. The period of three years is longer than those provided for by two of the most important Directives on consumer law adopted so far—the Directives on Unfair Terms in Consumer Contracts and on General Product Safety; eighteen months and two years respectively.[88] The three-year period provided by the Directive on Distance Contracts may be an attempt to cure the regular failure of Member States to transpose Directives on time. However, inefficiency rather than lack of time would seem the most likely explanation of failure to transpose legislation on time. Norway legislated in response to the Directive (as a member of the European Economic Area) almost immediately after its adoption.[89] Further, all Member States were aware of the possibility of legislation for many years, at least since the original proposal in 1992.

Finally, it should be mentioned that the Community has protected consumers' information (and quality) interests through the adoption of Directive

[86] In particular through the doctrines of: (a) direct effect, enabling individuals to rely directly on Community law against non- or mis-implementing Member States (Case 41/74, *Van Duyn v Home Office* [1974] ECR 1337); (b) state liability, enabling individuals to sue States for losses caused by failure properly to implement Community law (Cases C–6 & 9–90, *Francovich v Italy* [1991] ECR I–5357).

[87] It can be noted that subsequent Directives do not seem to have followed the Directive on Distance Contracts in this respect, eg the Directive on guarantees, note 45 above: 'The rights resulting from this Directive shall be exercised without prejudice to . . .' (Article 8).

[88] Directive 93/13/EC on Unfair Terms in Consumer Contracts and Directive 88/378/EC on General Product Safety.

[89] Consumer Contracts Annulment Form Order 1997 (May 2) [1997] Norsk Lovitund 858.

87/102 on consumer credit.[90] This provides for lenders to be liable along with sellers for goods and services supplied under a credit agreement of between 200 and 20,000 Euro where the good or service in question is not in conformity with the contract;[91] the effectiveness of this provision is clearly limited, as a great many e-commerce transactions will be worth less than 200 Euro.[92] Further, in order to exercise this right, the consumer must have first 'pursued' his remedies against the supplier and failed to obtain satisfaction.[93]

Secure Payment Mechanisms

Article 8 of the Directive on distance contracts provides consumers with protection against fraudulent use of their payment card.[94] Further the Commission in 1988 adopted a Recommendation on payments systems[95] which provides in particular that consumer liability for fraudulent use of a payment device is to be limited to 150 Euro prior to notification, except where the consumer is extremely negligent. This exception is far from clear and has the potential to confuse consumers as to the extent of their rights; it is at least possible to argue that a consumer sending payment device details over the Internet using unencrypted mail could be characterised as 'extremely negligent'. In reality, many sellers have made such requests and many consumers have complied. The payment device issuer is in a better position to control and

[90] Directive 87/102/EEC for the approximation of the laws, regulations and administrative provisions of the Member States concerning consumer credit, as amended by Directive 90/88/EEC, and Directive 98/7/EC. A revision process is underway, see European Commission DG Health and Consumer Protection, 'Discussion Paper for the amendment of Directive 87/102/EC concerning consumer credit', http://www.europa.eu.int/comm/consumers/cons_int/fina_serv/cons_directive/cons_cred1a_en.pdf. See also: the (US) Fair Credit and Billing Act 1975 and the Federal Electronic Funds Transfer Acts 1975 which provide consumers with protection over disputed billings, and lost or stolen cards (in the latter case liability is limited to $50 per credit card account and zero once the loss or theft is reported); s75 of the UK Consumer Credit Act 1975, applying to transactions over 100GBP.

[91] Article 11.

[92] It has been suggested that the lower limit was imposed in order to relieve sellers of the formalities imposed by the Directive, but that it could usefully be removed as regards connected lender liability, see G Howells and T Wilhemsson, *EC Consumer Law* (Aldershot, Dartmouth, 1997) at 197.

[93] Article 11(2)(e).

[94] 'Member States shall ensure that appropriate measures exist to allow a consumer:

> — to request cancellation of a payment where fraudulent use has been made of his payment card in connection with distance contracts covered by this Directive,
> — in the event of fraudulent use, to be recredited with the sums paid or have them returned.'

[95] Recommendation 88/950/EEC, largely superceding Recommendation 87/598/EEC on electronic payment. See generally, X Thunis, 'The Second European Recommendation Concerning Payment Systems: New Obligations for Card Issuers?' [1992] 3 *Journal of International Banking Law* 101, and Howells and Wilhemsson, note 92 above, at 214 and following.

to insure against misuse. A final criticism of the Recommendation is that research has shown that implementation of it has been deficient.[96]

Co-ordination

The Community has acted to ensure the co-ordination of the protection of consumers' fair trading interests through both soft- and hard- law measures. In relation to soft-law, the Commission is an active participant in the International Consumer Protection and Enforcement Network ('ICPEN'),[97] a network of consumer protection agencies designed to co-ordinate national bodies in their fight against illegal cross-border consumer marketing fraud. Its predecessor was the International Marketing Supervision Network ('IMSN') which suffered from incomplete coverage, even within industrialised countries; as at 1997 Italy had not joined because it did not have a public body with overall responsibility for consumer protection, Germany was represented by a non-governmental body with no executive power, and the United States ran into legal problems in becoming a member through restrictions on the ability of the Federal Trade Commission to provide information to foreign authorities.[98] Its principal activity is periodically to survey the Web to find illegal sites, an activity which is not always entirely successful—one 'sweep' conducted in 1997 resulted in 1100 suspect sites being contacted, yet only 28 per cent of these were subsequently removed or altered.[99] ICPEN is also hindered by poor international co-ordination. The more recently established International Society of Consumer and Competition Officials (ISCCO), which involves more countries than ICPEN, may help to solve some of these problems.[100]

In relation to hard-law, the Community has adopted a raft of measures aimed at ensuring consumers are protected in cross-border trade. First, as regards the law applicable to consumer contracts, the Rome Convention on the

[96] See J Mitchell and W Thomas, *Payment card terms and conditions in the European Union, A Survey of the Implementation of European Commission Recommendation 88/950/EEC on payment systems* (International Consumer Policy Bureau, 1995).

[97] www.icpen.org. ICPEN consists of twenty-nine member countries, including the EU member states, the United States, Canada, and Japan.

[98] *Per* Commission, *Proposal for a Council decision adopting a multiannual Community action plan on promoting safe use of the Internet*, COM(97) 582 at 17. The problems with the US stemmed from section 21 of the Federal Trade Commission Act, a provision originally enacted to protect the confidentiality of ongoing FTC investigations: R Starek, *Consumer Protection in the Age of Borderless Markets and the Information Revolution* (www.ftc.gov/speeches/starek/ausp.htm, 1995).

[99] *Per* http://www.imsnricc.org/imsn/activities.htm.

[100] See further www.iscco.org/what.html, identifying one of the objectives of the ISCCO as, 'the development of global consumer protection policies and practices'.

Law Applicable to Contractual Obligations (1980)[101] is commonly regarded as part of the *acquis communataire*, although formally an international treaty. It provides that,

> 'a choice of law made by the parties shall not have the result of depriving the consumer of the protection afforded to him by the mandatory rules of the law of the country in which he has his habitual residence:
>
> — if in that country the conclusion of the contract was preceded by a specific invitation addressed to him or by advertising, and he had there taken all the steps necessary on his part for the conclusion of the contract . . .'[102]

The (semi-official) Guiliano and Lagarde Report on the Convention is circumspect in relation to the impact of the above on cross-border contracts, stating that,

> 'the trader must have done certain acts such as advertising in the press, or on radio or television, or in the cinema or by catalogue aimed specifically at that country or he must have made business proposals through a middleman or by canvassing.'[103]

However, the rationale of the above can be taken to be that traders should not be unwittingly sucked into obligations derived from foreign rules. It is obvious to traders that transaction-enabled Web-sites create that risk. Those traders who view the risk as unacceptable can ask consumers to state their country of habitual residence and accept or reject them as appropriate. The Convention might be clearer as regards whether the consumer has to prove, and if so how, that he took all the steps necessary on his part for the conclusion of the contract in the country of his habitual residence. No instrument has been adopted in relation to the law applicable to non-contractual obligations, although the Commission in 2002 published a Proposal for a Regulation on the law applicable to non-contractual obligations ('Rome II').[104]

In addition to the Rome Convention, the *acquis communataire* includes four further instruments ensuring consumers' rights are effective across borders. First, in 1998 the Community adopted Directive 98/27 on cross-border

[101] The consolidated text of the Convention is published at OJ (1998) C27/34. See generally, R Plender and M Wilderspin, *European Contracts Convention* (Sweet & Maxwell, London, 2001). In 2002 the Commission proposed transforming it into a Regulation: Green Paper on the conversion of the Rome Convention of 1980 on the law applicable to contractual obligations into a Community instrument and its modernisation, COM(2002) 654 final. See generally, C Reifa, 'Article 5 of the Rome Convention on the Law Applicable to Contractual Obligations of 19 June 1980 and Consumer E-Contracts: The Need for Reform' (2004) 13 *Information & Communications Technology Law* 59.

[102] Article 5(2).

[103] OJ (1980) C282/1, 24.

[104] COM(2003) 427. The general rule proposed is that the applicable law be the law of the country in which the damage arises or is likely to arise, irrespective of the country in which the event giving rise to the damage occurred (Article 3(1)).

injunctions,[105] which is designed to facilitate cross-border action against those infringing Community consumer law; however the Directive does not encompass all breaches of consumer law, only those of the particular Community Directives it identifies.

Second, the Community recognised the localised nature of consumers' interest in redress through the adoption, under Title IV of the EC Treaty,[106] of Council Regulation 44/2001 on jurisdiction and the recognition and enforcement of judgments in civil and commercial matters ('the Brussels Regulation').[107] The Regulation is a modernisation of the Brussels Convention of 1968,[108] and provides that in respect of consumer contracts the consumer has the choice to sue either in the Member State in which she is domiciled or in the Member State in which the other party is domiciled, and that the consumer can only be sued in the Member State in which she is domiciled, where:

> 'the contract has been concluded with a person who pursues commercial or professional activities in the Member State of the consumer's domicile or, by any means, directs such activities to that Member State or to several States including that Member State, and the contract falls within the scope of such activities.' (Article 15(1)(c)).[109]

It is not clear what 'directs . . . activities' means, it might be interpreted in a restricted fashion, by analysing the 'main' directions of the Web-site, or it might be interpreted in an expansive fashion, analysing the 'direction' from the perspective of an individual consumer. For example, under the former interpretation a seller selling predominantly to the English-language market might

[105] Directive 98/27/EC on injunctions for the protection of consumers' interests.

[106] Title IV measures are not applicable in the UK, Ireland or Denmark unless those Member States opt-in. The UK and Ireland have opted in, whilst Denmark has not. The UK and Ireland have given notice of their intention to opt-in to all the Community's activities in the field of judicial co-operation in civil matters: Proposal, note 107 below, at 5.

[107] OJ 2001 L12/1. Denmark is not subject to the application of the Regulation, pursuant to Articles 1 and 2 of the Protocol on the position of Denmark annexed to the Treaty on European Union and to the EC Treaty establishing. See on the history of the Regulation: Proposal at COM(1999) 348 final, Council Working Party Report of April 1999, Council Document 7700/99, JUSTCIV 60; various position papers (of 1999) submitted to the European Commission on the issue can be found at: www.europa.eu.int/comm/scic/conference/991104/991104_info.htm. See also, L Gillies, 'A Review of the New Jurisdiction Rules for Electronic Consumer Contracts within the European Union' (2001) *Journal of Information Law & Technology* (http://elj.warwick.ac.uk/jilt/01-1/gillies.html).

[108] Consolidated version at OJ C1998/27. The Convention will remain in force as between Denmark and the Member States party to the Regulation (ie all other Member States), essentially the same rules are in force in EFTA states through the Lugano Convention 1988. As it is has now been largely superceded by the Brussels Regulation, the Brussels Convention will not be further referred to in any detail in this book.

[109] Article 4(1) provides an exception whereby if the defendant is not domiciled in a Member State then the jurisdiction of the courts of each Member State shall be determined by the courts of the Member State in question.

argue that its activities are 'directed' towards the UK and Ireland, sales elsewhere being incidental. Although use of the phrase 'by any means' militates in favour of the broad interpretation,[110] as does addressing the issue from the perspective of a concluded and individual contract, so that the seller must take steps to avoid directing its activities towards particular jurisdictions if it wishes to avoid them, consumer confidence would have benefited from this being made clear.

It does seem clear that a Web-site which does not offer consumers the possibility of contracting directly but does encourage consumers to use other routes to contract, eg e-mail or telephone, is caught by the provision as contracts so formed fall within 'the scope' of the Web-site. On the other hand, Web-sites detailing merely products and not means of buying the products (at a distance) cannot be said to be activities the scope of which includes contracts to buy the products (this is the opinion of the Council and Commission in their joint Declaration on Articles 15 and 73).[111]

The Brussels Regulation goes some way towards protecting the consumer interest in redress—to sue or be sued in a foreign country involves disproportionate costs and burden for a consumer, less so for sellers. The Regulation makes provision for the issuance of a standard form certificate of judgment (Article 54 and Annex V), which benefits from 'fast-track' procedures for recognition and enforcement.[112]

Third, Parliament and Council would appear, as at August 2004, to be about to adopt a Regulation on Enforcement Cooperation, having reached agreement on the Commission's Proposal on the same at first reading.[113] This will create an EU-wide network of national enforcement authorities capable of taking co-ordinated action against rogue traders who run cross border scams, parallel to similar networks which exist in the areas of customs, taxation, competition and financial services. The Regulation will require each Member State

[110] It has been suggested that such a wide phrase imposes some sort of strict liability on e-commerce businesses, ie in the absence of fraud on the part of the consumer, if a business contracts with the consumer, then the consumer acquires the right to sue in the State of her domicile, see M Pullen, *On the Proposals to Adopt the Amended Brussels Convention and the Draft Rome II Convention as EU Regulations pursuant to Article 65 of the Amsterdam Treaty* (www.ilpf.org/confer/present99/pullen_posit.htm, 1999). See also Council and Commission *Statement on Articles 15 and 73* (europa.eu.int/comm/justice_home/unit/civil_en/htm).

[111] Available at www.europa.eu.int/comm/justice_home/unit/civil_en.htm. See also the US case of *Inset Sys Inc. v Instruction Set Inc* 973 F Supp 161 (D Conn, 1996) in which it was held that online advertising together with a free telephone number was sufficient contact with the court's state to confer jurisdiction.

[112] Review of a certificate can be made only on limited grounds, namely: where it is manifestly contrary to public policy, where it was given in default of appearance, where it is irreconcilable with an existing judgment given in a dispute between the same parties whether in the Member State in which recognition is sought or in certain circumstances, in a third state: Article 34.

[113] COM(2003) 443; Commission Press Release IP/04/655 of 18th May 2004.

to designate a public enforcement authority to be part of a mutual assistance network. Each competent authority will be able to call on other members of the network for assistance in investigating a possible breach of consumer laws, finding information or, ultimately, ensuring a rogue trader is stopped.

Fourth, it can further be noted that the Community is an active participant in the Hague Conference's work on its Draft Convention on Jurisdiction and Enforcement.[114]

What the Community has not in particular, but might have, done, is to establish a regime of joint liability between seller and manufacturer for goods not in conformity with the contract. In many cases, this would enable consumers buying abroad via e-commerce to obtain redress for non-conformity at home, via the manufacturer. As Professor Thomas Wilhelmsson has commented, 'The consumer is more confident when he can discuss with an easily accessible . . . counterparty.'[115] Furthermore, such liability would reflect the modern reality that in respect of many types of goods consumers' purchasing decisions are based on trust in the manufacturer, the identity of the seller being often incidental. Despite the European Commission suggesting such joint liability in 1993,[116] and its existence in various Member States,[117] the Community has not instituted any such system.

Observations

The above analysis shows serious flaws in the Community's protection of consumers' fair trading interest. The Community has instituted a system of home country control of marketing which disables Member States' ability to protect their consumer-citizens from unfair marketing practices and which creates downward pressure on national marketing rules. The general Community definition of 'consumer' does not correspond with the need to protect parties with weak bargaining power vis-à-vis the seller. The Directive on distance contracts excludes contracts for financial services without a justifiable reason (although the Directive on the distance marketing of financial services has now

[114] See generally on the progress of the Draft Convention, www.hcch.net. The Commission currently has observer status at the Hague Conference, although after the entry into force of the Treaty of Amsterdam and the communitarisation of the area of judicial co-operation in civil matters, much of the Hague work now falls under Community competence, and it seems likely that the Community will shortly become a member of the Hague Conference.

[115] 'The Abuse of the 'Confident Consumer' as a Justification for EC Consumer Law' (2004) 27 *Journal of Consumer Policy* 317 at 333.

[116] *Green Paper on guarantees for consumer goods and after-sales services*, COM(93) 509.

[117] The Green Paper notes France, Belgium and Luxembourg, at 87.

filled the gap), and fails to 'ring-fence' consumers' advance payments. Its provisions on prior information are somewhat neutered by the lack of direct protection for consumers prejudiced by breach.

The Community's facilitation of the cross-border protection of consumers' rights through the Rome Convention, the Brussels Regulation and the Directive on Injunctions is undoubtedly positive. However, these measures are no substitute for adequate substantive protection of consumers' interests. Indeed, the Community may there be in breach of Article 95(3) of the Treaty, which states that, in measures adopted under Article 95 the Community institutions are to aim at, and seek to achieve, a 'high level' of protection in consumer law. Further, the Community has not moved towards a system of manufacturer liability, which would often enable consumers buying abroad via e-commerce to obtain redress for non-conformity at home. It is suggested that this issue is critical in giving the average consumer the confidence to participate in the electronic marketplace.

The area of consumers' privacy interests will now be assessed.

3

Consumers II—Privacy Interests

Threats to Consumers' Privacy Interests

'Access to digital mobile networks has become available and affordable for a large public. These digital networks have large capacities and possibilities for processing personal data. The successful cross-border development of these services is partly dependent on the confidence of users that their privacy will not be at risk.' *Preamble to Directive 2002/58/EC on privacy and electronic communications, Recital 5.*

'It is essential . . . to assure personal privacy in the networked environment if people are to feel comfortable doing business,' *US President Clinton and Vice-President Gore, A Framework for Global Electronic Commerce.*[1]

The online threats to consumers' privacy interests are driven by the interests of data processors in collecting large amounts of personal data, by the computing power which is an integral part of the electronic marketplace,[2] and by the particular technical features of the Internet.

[1] White House Information Infrastructure Task Force, 1998, www.iitf.nist.gov/eleccomm/ecomm.htm.

[2] See generally, J Rosenberg, *The Death of Privacy* (New York, Random House, 1969), which detailed the growing capacity of computers to build profiles of people from items of data which had previously been entirely separate. Other landmarks in the analysis of privacy include: M Baker and A Westin, *Databanks in a Free Society: Computers, Record-Keeping and Privacy* (New York, Quadrangle Books, 1972) and D Burnham, *The Rise of the Computer State: A Chilling Account of the Computer's Threat to Society* (New York, Random House, 1983). Contrast A Etzioni, *The Limits of Privacy* (New York, Basic Books, 1999), who argues that society's right to

As regards consumers' interest in consent to collection of personal data, the ability of processors to surreptitiously record consumers' browsing behaviour poses two particular challenges:

— Computers linked to the Net have attached Internet Protocol addresses, and those addresses which are temporary can often be linked to a specific subscriber, through data held by the service provider; the identities of owners of permanent Internet Protocol addresses are generally publicly available.[3]
— Web-sites may capture a wide range of information from visitors' computers including service provider, clock time, e-mail address,[4] file-names and other sites visited; all or some of this information might be capable of personally identifying that individual.[5]

Further, the current Hypertext Transfer Protocol allows Web-sites surreptitiously to place on consumers' computers files known as 'cookies', which are capable of identifying consumers individually, and of tracking their online behaviour.[6] Individual identification is dependent upon collation with other information. Cookies have benefits for consumers in as much as they can speed the verification of identity, but are often used without consent. The files themselves are permanent .txt files generally readable only by the site which placed them (although consumers with the necessary technical knowledge can also read them). Clearly, browsing habits can reveal highly sensitive data, for example where a user visits particular religious sites on a regular basis. A failed attempt was made in 1997 within the Internet Engineering Task Force to exclude the use of cookies via change to the hypertext transfer protocol.[7] Their use is widespread—partly through the use of cookies, *DoubleClick* had by February 2000 managed to build up 100 million consumer-profiles.[8]

information about its members generally outweighs the right of individuals to privacy. These learned books have been paralleled by a number of high-profile cases of data abuse, one of the most famous being the release of the video rental records of rejected US Supreme Court-nominee Robert Bork, whose video rental records were released during his confirmation hearings (Congress subsequently adopted a law outlawing such activity, the Video Privacy Act, 18 USC. 2710–11).

[3] See generally http://www.internic.net/.

[4] Due to advances in browser technology, this is now rare.

[5] See generally, Commission Working Party Recommendation 1/99, 'Invisible and automatic processing of personal data on the Internet performed by software and hardware' (www.europa.eu.int/comm/en/internal_market/, 23 February 1999).

[6] See generally, S Gauthronet and F Nathan, 'Online services and data protection and the protection of privacy' (Commission, www.europa.eu.int/comm/dg15/en/media/dataprot, 1998) at 28–33.

[7] See Request for Comments 2109, www.ietf.org.

[8] Electronic Privacy Information Centre Complaint to the Federal Trade Commission, *In the Matter of DoubleClick Inc., Complaint and Request for Injunction, Request for Investigation and for Other Relief* (www.epic.org/privacy/internet/ftc/DCLK_complaint.pdf) at 4. 'Cookie' profiles can be accessed online (as they can offline) via 'look up' service-providers such as digdirt.com.

It is difficult to determine the precise extent to which personal data is processed without consent for the simple reason that the processing activities of private entities are not generally made public. No empirical survey has ever managed to delve into the critical question of whether companies follow their stated practices.[9] However, it is clear from the following surveys that a significant proportion of Web-sites collect personal data without giving any kind of notice to that effect:

Georgetown University Survey 1999:[10]

— whilst 93 per cent of the busiest sites (world-wide) collected personal data from consumers, only 14 per cent of the same sample fully disclosed their information practices.[11]

FTC survey 2000:[12]

— 41 per cent of a random sample of Web-sites did not respect the principles of notice and choice.[13]

— 80 per cent of the sample did not respect the principles of notice, consent, access and security.[14]

A specific problem in respect of consent to processing is that of bulk unsolicited commercial e-mail ('spam').[15] The history of this problem is usually traced to a mass e-mail sent out in 1994 to every Usenet newsgroup in the world by two US lawyers, Lawrence Canter and Martha Seigel, advertising advice in relation to the popular Green Card Lottery run each year by the US.[16] Spam has since become a self-contained industry, which includes the use of off-the-shelf spamming software ('spamware') and specialised spamming services.

Spamware is of two types, the first designed to harvest e-mail addresses and the second to distribute spam. Harvesting programs, such as Atomic Harvester 3 (available online for $179),[17] usually search Web-sites located through

[9] As pointed out by the Center for Democracy and Technology in, 'Behind the Numbers: Privacy Practices on the Web' (http://www.cdt.org/privacy/990727privacy.shtml, 1999).

[10] www.msb.edu/faculty/culnanm/gippshome.html. The survey was conducted on the 100 busiest sites world-wide and a random sample of 361 sites world-wide.

[11] Executive summary at 1.

[12] *Privacy Online: Fair Information Practices in the Electronic Marketplace* (http://www.ftc.gov/os/2000/05/index.htm#22, May 2000). The survey was conducted on the 100 busiest US sites and a random sample of 335 US sites.

[13] At 14.

[14] At 13.

[15] The term 'spam' comes from a pork and ham luncheon meat of the same name, commonly part of British school meals in years gone by and ridiculed in a famous Monty Python comedy sketch. For a list of cases from around the world on spam see www.jmls.edu/cyber/cases/spam.html, and see generally, L Edwards, 'Canning the Spam': Is There a Case for Legal Control of Junk Electronic Mail?, in L Edwards and C Waelde (eds), *Law and the Internet* (Oxford, Hart Publishing, 2000).

[16] See their book, *How to make a fortune on the information superhighway* (Los Angeles, Noel Products, 1994).

[17] http://www.stratton.zen.co.uk/dtsiv/. Neither this program nor other spamware appears to be available except through online downloading.

keywords entered by the spammer and fed into search engines.[18] Distribution software, such as SpeedSendMailer,[19] enable spammers to use their own PCs as servers, thus doing away with the problems associated with using an ISP's bandwidth. SpeedSendMailer allows random selection of the 'from' field and subject line, and has a mailing speed of 100–3000+ messages per minute, depending on the size of the e-mail and the capacities of the CPU and modem.

In the field of spamming service-providers, e-mail address brokers such as ListKingPro[20] can be easily found on the Web. These offer e-mail address lists as either one-off purchases or on a monthly-paid subscription basis. For example, ListKingPro offers the use of 50,000 'clean' addresses once per month for $99 a month, and 125,000 for $175 a month.

Spam wastes consumers' time and money. It is particularly burdensome in the latter respect for those consumers who pay telephone connection charges as they download their mail. Further, e-mail boxes with restricted capacity may become full of spam and unable to accept more important messages. Spam is often used to promote services of dubious legitimacy; one e-mail based scam involved sending consumers an e-mail which falsely 'confirmed' a recent purchase made by them; when those users tried to reply to that e-mail, their message was rejected, leaving them with only a telephone number, which connected to a premium-rate sex line based in the Dominican Republic; the revenue stream from this scam was traced and found to lead to an agent in Gibraltar.[21] Despite it being clear that consumers have long objected to being sent spam,[22] it is a continuing and serious problem.

A final problem with consent to online data processing exists in relation to children. Minors have in the past been largely out of the reach of data processors, yet e-commerce brings the two into direct contact and has a concomitant impact on parents' confidence. An FTC survey of 1998 found that whilst 89 per cent of sites directed at children collected personal information, only 1 per cent required prior parental consent.[23] One site in the United States—*Kids.Com*—offered children access to a free games site in return for personal details includ-

[18] *Ibid.*

[19] $149 at http://www.bulk-email-supermarket.com/speedsendmailer.htm (based in Utah).

[20] http://www.listkingpro.com.

[21] Testimony of Eileen Harrington of the Federal Trade Commission to hearings of the same on, 'In the Matter of the Global E-Marketplace' (www.ftc.gov/bcp/icpw/index.htm, June 1999) at 164 and following. See also the details of spam advertising fraudulent investments given in J Cella and J Stark, 'SEC Enforcement and the Internet: Meeting the Challenge of the Next Millennium' (1997) 52 *Business Law* 815 at 832.

[22] In 1997 it topped the list of complaints made by customers of AOL: per Jill Lesser, FTC Workshop on Consumer Information Privacy (www.ftc.gov/bcp/privacy /wkshp97/volume3.pdf, June 1997) at 51.

[23] Federal Trade Commission, *Privacy Online: A Report to Congress* (www.ftc.gov/reports/privacy3/index.htm) at 4.

ing birth dates, career plans, their own e-mail addresses and those of their parents (these practices were stopped further to the enactment of the Children's Online Privacy Protection Act 1998).[24]

In relation to security, the very communications technology which enables legitimate data processors to collect data, also facilitates fraudulent access to databases. There has been a series of cases in which such access has been reported and there are likely many more cases which have gone unreported given that it is not in a processor's interest to reveal that its security systems have been breached. The *FTC 2000* study cited above found that 45 per cent of sampled Web-sites did not post any notice regarding security, and furthermore 57 per cent did not offer consumers the opportunity to access their data.[25]

It will now be considered whether self-help might be able to neutralise these threats to consumers' privacy interests.

Self-help as a Solution?

> 'We believe that the private effort of industry working in cooperation with consumer groups is preferable to government regulation . . .' *US President Clinton and Vice-President Gore, A Framework for Global Electronic Commerce.*

Various policy actors—including business organisations,[26] the US government[27] and the OECD[28]—have suggested that self-help has an important role

[24] See http://www.ftc.gov/opa/1999/9910/childfinal.htm. The Act outlawed the collection of data from children under 13 without verifiable parental consent. See generally: R Starek, 'The ABCs at the FTC: Marketing and Advertising to Children' (www.ftc.gov/speeches/starek/minnfinn.htm, July 1997).

[25] At 19.

[26] See eg Global Business Dialogue on Electronic Commerce (GBDe): 'Due to the global, decentralized, open, rapidly-evolving, and immature nature of electronic networks in general and the Internet in particular, we believe that protection of individually identified or identifiable data (Personal Data) is most effectively achieved through private-sector leadership', *Protection of Personal Data* (www.toshiba.co.jp/gbde-prv/final1.htm (no longer available), 1999) at III(1). The GBDe does not spell out the logic of this deduction. Also the Online Privacy Alliance, which has stated that it 'will lead and support self-regulatory initiatives that create an environment of trust and that foster the protection of individuals' privacy online and in electronic commerce' (www.privacyalliance.com/mission, at 1999).

[27] Note 23 above, also: the US National Telecommunications and Information Administration (NTIA), *Safeguarding Telecommunications-Related Personal Information* (1995); US Department of Commerce, *Privacy and Self-help in the Information Age* (www.ntia.doc.gov/reports/privacy/selfreg1.htm, 1997). Contrast: American Civil Liberties Union, *Take Back Your Data* (www.aclu.org/action/tbyd.html, 1998).

[28] 'Different effective approaches to privacy protection developed by Member countries, including the adoption and implementation of laws or industry self-help, can work together to achieve effective privacy protection on global networks . . . [T]here is a need for global co-operation and the necessity of industry and business taking a key role, in co-operation with

to play in solving the the problems described above. As in the field of consumers' fair trading interests, the touchstone of self-help is the trusted third party, both in certifying privacy-friendly Web-sites via 'trustmarks' and 'privacy seals', and in producing privacy-protecting software. The existence of privacy policies cannot in itself be considered a genuine avenue of self-help given that, first, it is unreasonable to expect the average consumer to read those policies and second, no study has ever shown the extent to which privacy policies are followed. There are certainly examples of companies not following their own stated policies: in 1998 it became clear that although *GeoCities* promised consumers that it would not pass their data on to any third party without their consent, it did in fact do so routinely.[29]

It can further be pointed out that children's inability to appreciate the nature of their right to privacy means that self-help is a non-issue as far as children themselves are concerned, although of course that may not be the case for those responsible for them. The roles of trustmarks and privacy-protecting software will now be considered.

Trustmarks

> 'Reliable trustmark schemes can help to identify enterprises that have agreed to meet certain standards or guidelines when doing business online.' *Union of Industrial and Employers' Confederation of Europe, European Consumers' Organisation (BEUC), Agreement on a European Framework for e-commerce trustmark schemes.*[30]

The aim of the privacy trustmark is to reassure individuals that a particular site or company conforms to certain standards of privacy practice; the best-known example is TRUSTe,[31] established in 1996 by the Electronic Frontier Foundation[32] and the CommerceNet Consortium.[33] This mark covers a number of the world's most popular Web-sites, including Netscape, AOL, Yahoo and Infoseek. It is awarded to sites which tell visitors:

consumers and governments . . .' *Ministerial Declaration on the Protection of Privacy on Global Networks* (www.oecd.org/dsti/sti/it/secur/, 1998) at 2.

[29] See FTC, *GeoCities Agreement and Consent Order,* File No. 9823015 (www.ftc.gov/os/1998/–9808/geo–ord.htm, 1998); FTC, *Analysis of Proposed Consent Order to Aid Public Comment* (www.ftc.gov/os/1998/9808/9823015.-ana.htm, 1998).

[30] 2001, http://docshare.beuc.org/Contents/Contents.

[31] www.truste.org. Other examples include the Better Business Bureau Online mark used in the United States, see www.bbbonline.com/businesses/privacy/index.htm, and the TrustUK mark established by the Consumer's Association and the Alliance of Electronic Business in the UK (www.trustuk.org.uk).

[32] A not-for-profit, individual-membership organisation open to all, committed to ensuring respect for individuals' rights in new media, www.eff.org.

[33] A grouping of commercial operators on the Net, www.commerce.net.

— what personal information is being gathered,
— how it will be used,
— with whom it will be shared,
— whether or not the user has an option to control dissemination, and
— how their data is (a) kept secure, (b) can be accessed and (c) can be corrected.[34]

This list, which is typical of other trustmark's policies,[35] corresponds *broadly* to the constituent elements of consumers' privacy interest as set out in chapter 1 above. (However, this correspondence is not absolute, which shows the need for regulation.) Trustmarks do not satisfy consumers' interest in accountability—Web-sites are accountable to the mark itself, but this is of no succour to the individual data subject whose interests are prejudiced. As with fair trading marks, if an individual sees a mark and enters a site relying on it, but the site then does not follow the policies behind the mark, the individual is left unprotected. Such an occurrence may be beyond the control of those who instituted the original policy, such as where a company enters bankruptcy proceedings; a concrete example is the bankruptcy of Toysmart in 2000, subsequent to which the Federal Trade Commission had to intervene to stop the administrator selling Toysmart's customer list.[36]

Further, trustmarks do not cover all Web-sites—the FTC 2000 survey noted above found that only 45 per cent of the most popular sites bore a trustmark.[37] Nor can trustmarks pretend to universality amongst consumers, not all of whom can be expected to understand what a trustmark means.

Nor are trustmarks financially independent of the businesses they are supposed to police. TRUSTe is largely dependent upon the financial support of subscribing Web-sites,[38] and BBBOnline entirely so.[39] The operation of trustmarks in practice would seem to reflect this lack of independence, as illustrated by two cases involving TRUSTe. In November 1999 it became clear that *RealNetworks*, a TRUSTe-certified site, was collecting personally-identifiable information from visitors without giving notice of that fact, in clear breach of TRUSTe's policies. The company gave away audio software, without informing consumers that the software surreptitiously collected information on their online behaviour and transmitted that information back to *RealNetworks*.[40] Although *RealNetworks* apologised to consumers and agreed to change its

[34] www.truste.org/about/about_truste.html.

[35] The Web-sites of TrustUK and BBBOnline, note 31 above, reveal that their policies are broadly the same.

[36] *World Data Protection Report*, January 2001, 13.

[37] Note 12 above, at 20.

[38] See www.truste.org/about/.

[39] See www.bbbonline.org.

[40] WIRED News, 'Real Damage Control—Again' (www.wired.com/news/technology/0,1282,32350,00.html, 6 November 1999).

policy, TRUSTe invoked no sanction against it.[41] The apology of *RealNetworks* is an interesting indicator of commercial acceptance of the legitimacy of consumers' online privacy interest—the apology did not suggest that consumers' general expectation of privacy was unreasonable, nor that they had given away this right in return for free software, nor that it was in consumers' interests that data be collected upon them.

The second case involved Microsoft, another of TRUSTe's sponsors, which in May 1999 admitted using software registration to obtain hardware identification information from individual's computers, again without giving notice of that fact.[42] The registration process appeared to offer consumers the choice of transferring or withholding the information, but in fact transferred the information whatever choice was made. As in the *RealNetworks* case, TRUSTe failed to take action,[43] its justification being that the sequence of events did not take place as part of visiting Microsoft's Web-site. This seems a narrow interpretation of its role, and not one geared towards generating consumer confidence. Indeed, as at August 2004 the TRUSTe site contained no indication of any site which had had its licence to use the mark withdrawn.

It would thus seem that trustmarks alone cannot ensure the protection of consumers' interests. In particular, they are not able to offer remedies if data processors break their promises. Further, they have an in-built bias towards processors and against data subjects. Trustmarks may in fact sometimes have a negative impact upon consumers' privacy, in serving as superficial attractions for those who do not understand how their privacy might be invaded.

Given that trustmarks cannot entirely resolve the threats to consumers' interests, the following section discusses the extent to which software can.

Software

In respect of data-collecting Web-sites, user-installed software allows individuals to screen sites for privacy protection. The focus of attention in this field is the *Platform for Privacy Preferences* ('P3P'),[44] developed by the World Wide Web Consortium.[45] Via their browsers, consumers can use P3P to specify what information they are willing to make available, eg name, e-mail address etc, and

[41] See www.qlinks.net/items/qlitem5432.htm, 11 November 1999; www.currents.net/newstoday/99/11/09/news11.html, 9 November 1999.

[42] See WIRED News, 'Microsoft off TRUSTe's hook' (http://www.wired.com/news/technology/0,1282,18639,00.html, 22 March 1999).

[43] *Ibid.*

[44] The latest version can be found at http://www.w3.org/P3P/. See generally Commission Working Party on Data Protection Opinion 1/98, *Platform for Privacy Preferences and the Open Profiling Standard* (www.europa.eu.int/comm/dg15/en/media/dataprot/index.htm).

[45] www.w3.org. The World Wide Web Consortium is a grouping of 400 member-companies which aims to develop common protocols to ensure the inter-operability of the Web.

to whom, eg an individual Web-site, delivery agents, unspecified third parties. The consumer's browser interacts with Web-sites to determine whether they comply with the specified requirements and warns the consumer if this is not the case. The consumer can then decide whether to continue, or to leave the site.

P3P has evident attractions. It protects consumers' interests in notice and consent. It is user-driven and thus avoids the lack of independence which is inherent in some trustmarks, and consumers can tailor it to their own individual standards.[46] Notwithstanding these attractions, P3P has three significant drawbacks. First, its protective capacity is inherently dependent upon consumers' technical sophistication. Those who do not know of the existence of threats to their online privacy, or do not know that there is software capable of protecting them, cannot be protected by it. Second, P3P presents problems in relation to enforcement, as it sets only pre-collection standards. As with trustmarks, P3P comports no means of ensuring that Web-sites act according to their promises. Software cannot provide a remedy to the consumer who gives out personal data on the strength of promises which are subsequently broken. Third, although P3P is universal in the sense that consumers can tailor it to their individual needs, in practical terms the use of P3P shuts off access to sites which are not P3P-compliant, which is currently most of them (the World Wide Web Consortium's list of P3P-compliant sites as of July 2004 contained only 500 or so sites).[47] This is a serious discouragement to those consumers anxious to protect their privacy.[48]

Although P3P is currently in operation and arguably fulfils a role for some, the above shows that it is not in a position to ensure protection of all consumers' interests.

In respect of software and the specific problem of spam, users can install software which analyses incoming e-mail against certain criteria, and either blocks the message or allows it through on that basis. Examples of such software include *SpamNet*[49] and *SpamSleuth*.[50] Although in independent reviews these products have generally proved effective,[51] the downside for consumers is of course that they cost money (typically about 30 euros).

[46] Contrast J Reidenberg, 'Lex Informatica: The Formulation of Information Policy Rules Through Technology' (1998) 76 *Texas Law Review* 553, who argues that P3P might create lock-in, ie downward pressure on privacy standards, at 586 and following.

[47] http://www.w3.org/P3P/compliant_sites.

[48] P Schwartz, 'Privacy and Democracy in Cyberspace' (1999) 52 *Vanderbilt Law Review* 1609 at 1695, (also available at: http://www.wcbcourses.com/wcb/schools/LEXIS/law08/pschwartz/3/files/VAND-SCHWARTZ.PDF). See also the similar criticisms of the Electronic Privacy Information Centre in, *Pretty Poor Privacy* (www.epic.org/reports/prettypoorprivacy. htm, June 2000) at 9.

[49] www.cloudmark.com.

[50] www.bluesquirrel.com.

[51] See eg the review of *SpamSleth* at http://www.sharewarejunkies.com/02zwd9/spam_sleuth.htm.

Despite the continuing pleas of proponents,[52] it is clear that self-help of itself is not sufficient to protect consumers' interests, in particular those in access and in redress, and more generally in respect of consumers who are not technologically knowledgeable. The following section will consider the extent to which Community regulation fills the gaps left by self-help.

Community Regulation

> 'Whereas data-processing systems are designed to serve man; whereas they must, whatever the nationality or residence of natural persons, respect . . . the right to privacy, and contribute to economic and social progress, trade expansion and the well-being of individuals.' *Recital 2 of the Preamble to the Privacy Directive.*[53]

In respect of privacy protection generally, the Community has directed its energies towards the development of a public law framework rather than towards supporting self-help. However, Privacy Directive 95/46 does make provision for the Member States and the Commission to encourage the drawing up of codes of conduct,[54] and the Community has contributed to the OECD's work on privacy, in particular the 1980 Guidelines on the Protection of Privacy and Transborder Flows of Personal Data and the 1998 Ministerial Declaration on the Protection of Privacy on Global Networks.[55]

The Community's public law framework for privacy is centred around the 1995 Privacy Directive,[56] the implementation date for which was 24 October

[52] A good example is William Kennard, then Chairman of the US Federal Communications Commission, who said in May 2000 that, given the incentives industry had to create a secure environment, government should 'give self-regulation a chance' (May 2000) *Electronic Commerce and Law Report* 591 at 591—this comment was made some considerable number of years after the incentives came into existence. Further, within the US itself, research into off-line privacy has shown poor levels of compliance with self-regulatory standards: J Reidenberg and P Schwartz, *Data Privacy Law* (Charlottesville, Michie, 1998) at 308–9, dealing in particular with the Direct Marketing Association's Code of Practice.

[53] Directive 95/46/EC on the protection of physical persons as regards the processing of personal data and the free movement of data, OJ 1995 L281/31.

[54] Note 53 above, Article 27(1) 'The Member States and the Commission shall encourage the drawing up of codes of conduct intended to contribute to the proper implementation of the national provisions adopted by the Member States, pursuant to this Directive, taking account of the specific features of the various sectors . . .'

[55] See the conclusions of the Ottawa Conference on Electronic Commerce October 1998, available from http://www.ottawaoecdconference.org/. The work of the OECD in this regard is ongoing, see http://www.oecd.org/dsti/sti/it/secur/.

[56] Note 53 above. A report has been produced on the application of the Directive (and corresponding national law) to online services: J Reidenberg and P Schwartz, *Data Protection Law and On-line Services: Regulatory Responses* (www.europa.eu.int/comm/dg15/en/media/dataprot, 1999). See generally on the Directive: A White, 'Control of Transborder Data Flow: Reactions to the European Data Protection Directive' (1997) 5 *International Journal of Information &*

1998, a date which only four Member States met.[57] It is clear from Article 1 that the Directive is based upon a notion of privacy as a fundamental right: 'Member States shall protect the fundamental rights and freedoms of natural persons, and in particular their right to privacy with respect to the processing of personal data.' In addition to the Privacy Directive, the Community has also adopted Directive 2002/58 on e-privacy,[58] replacing Directive 97/66 concerning the processing of personal data and the protection of privacy in the telecommunications sector.[59] The Privacy Directive provides a basic framework, on which the Directive on e-privacy builds in the specific context of electronic communications. As will be discussed below, these Directives offer *broad* protection for most of consumers' privacy interest. However, in the online environment there are question marks over the scope of the Directives.

The Privacy Directive applies to the processing, wholly or partly by automated means, of personal data, which is defined as meaning any information relating to someone who can be identified, directly or indirectly, in particular by reference to an identification number or to one or more factors specific to his physical, physiological, mental, economic, cultural or social identity.[60] Yet it is not clear whether a data subject is 'identifiable' by virtue of a processor collating its data with data held by another processor—a common possibility online.

A further lack of clarity is evident in that the Privacy Directive mandates Member States to apply corresponding national provisions where data processing is carried out in the context of the activities of an establishment of the 'controller'[61] on the territory of the Member State.[62] It is not clear what constitutes such an 'establishment' in the transient world of the Internet, and research has shown national laws to be on diverging paths in interpreting this provision.[63] Recital 20 does provide some protection for consumers where the processor is established in a third country:

Technology 230; Article 29 Committee of Directorate-General Internal Market of the Commission, *Privacy on the Internet: an integrated EU approach* (http://www.europa.eu.int/comm/internal_market/en/media/dataprot/wpdocs/wp37en.pdf, November 2000).

[57] Commissions Press Release IP/03/697 of 16/05/2003.

[58] OJ 2002 L201/37, available from http://europa.eu.int/comm/internal_market/privacy/index_en.htm. See also the Proposal, COM(2000) 385.

[59] OJ 1998 L24/1.

[60] Article 2(a).

[61] 'The natural or legal person, public authority, agency or other body which alone or jointly with others determines the purposes and means of the processing of personal data', Article 2(d). This is arguably a conceptualisation more suited to the era of mainframes rather than of distributed networks, see R Litan and P Swire, *None of Your Business: World Data Flows, Electronic Commerce, and the European Privacy Directive* (Washington DC, Brookings Institution Press, 1998) at 50.

[62] Article 4(1)(a).

[63] See J Reidenberg and P Schwartz, *Data Privacy Law* (Charlottesville, Michie, 1996) at 32.

> 'Whereas the fact that that the processing of data is carried out by a person established in a third country must not stand in the way of the protection of individuals provided for in this Directive; whereas in these cases, the processing should be governed by the law of the Member State in which the means used are located, and there should be guarantees to ensure that the rights and obligations provided for in this Directive are respected in practice.'

The Article 29 Working Party's *Working document on determining the international application of EU data protection law to personal data processing on the Internet by non-EU based web sites,*[64] opines that 'means' in Recital 20 above includes users' PCs.[65]

Neither of the Directives makes special provision for the problems noted above concerning children's online privacy. In particular, neither recognises the potential problems associated with unsupervised contact between children and marketers. In this the Community compares poorly with the US, which in 1998 adopted the Children's Online Privacy Protection Act.[66]

In respect of notice and consent, the Privacy Directive provides:

> **Notice:** 'Data shall be . . . collected for specified, explicit and legitimate purposes . . .', Article 6(1)(b).
> **Consent:** 'Personal data may be processed only if:
> (a) the data subject has unambiguously given his consent; or
> (b)–(e) [various specific circumstances are given[67] which negate the need for unambiguous consent]; or
> (f) processing is necessary for the purposes of the legitimate interests pursued by the controller or by the third party or parties to whom the data are disclosed, except where such interests are overridden by the interests for fundamental rights and freedoms of the data subject which require protection under Article 1.' (Article 7).

Articles 19(1)(b) and (d) add in respect of notice that processors must supply information regarding the purpose or purposes of the processing and the recipients or categories of recipient to whom the data might be disclosed. However, no guidance is given as to whether data processors wishing to transfer data to third parties can satisfy the 'purpose' provision simply by stating that data will be processed for commercial purposes, or whether they need to state that the data might be disclosed to those who have a commercial interest in it.

64 (2002) http://europa.eu.int/comm/internal_market/privacy/docs/wpdocs/2002/wp56_en.pdf. See also L Bygrave, 'Determining Applicable Law Pursuant to European Data Protection Legislation' (2000) 16 *Computer Law and Security Report* 252; D Scherzer, 'EU Regulation of Processing of Personal Data by Wholly Non-Europe-Based Websites' (2003) 25(7) *European Intellectual Property Review* 292.

65 At 9.

66 Note 24 above.

67 Relating to the performance of a contract, the processor's compliance with a legal obligation, protecting the vital interests of the data subject, and the performance of a task carried out in the public interest.

Consumers may not understand the consequences of these statements, in particular that 'disclosure of data to others' will often result in subsequent contact.

Furthermore, although Article 7(a) above requires that the collection of data generally be subject to the 'unambiguous consent' of the data subject, it is not clear what this means in an online context. It would seem that a data processor can satisfy the requirement simply by giving notice via a link to a Web page, which most consumers will never read. There is no explicit requirement that the consumer actually be made aware of collection via prominent lettering or an 'opt-in' scheme.[68] As noted above, Web-sites are capable of collecting personal data in an invisible fashion. It is submitted that consumer confidence would be maximised if explicit consent were required through opt-in.

A further alternative to ensure effective consent would be a provision obliging those who use personal data to contact consumers to identify their source. This would have the benefit of increasing the transparency of data processing and of enabling consumers better to control their privacy and to see the 'circular' potential of data processing (ie collection can often result in subsequent contact). Thus a consumer contacted for marketing purposes by Company X might be informed that her details were obtained from Company Y, which received her consent to the disclosure of her data on Date Z, and the consumer could be given the opportunity to revoke that consent. Another issue is the length of time consumers consent to their data being held. Anecdotal evidence suggests that in the UK at least consumers feel frustration at the length of time data processors hold data for marketing purposes—there would appear to be a preference for data to be held for a certain period of time rather than indefinitely.

Both the Privacy Directive and the Directive on e-privacy make provision as to security:

> 'The controller must implement appropriate technical and organizational measures to protect personal data from accidental or unlawful destruction or accidental loss, alteration, unauthorized disclosure or access.' (Article 17, Privacy Directive).

> 'The provider . . . must take appropriate technical and organisational measures to safeguard security of its services . . . Having regard to the state of the art and the cost of their implementation, these measures shall ensure a level of security appropriate to the risk presented.' (Article 4(1), Directive on e-privacy).

These obligations support consumer confidence, as their flexibility enables regulatory standards to evolve in tandem with the practices of data processors. However, consumers are unlikely ever to know if security has been breached,

[68] Contrast for example s44 of the UK's Consumer Credit Act 1974 which does provide for specific requirements of form for the notification of annual percentage interest rates.

and in that light it is worthwhile repeating the point made above about mandating information regarding the source of personal data used in marketing communications, ie such identification would act as a check on illicit acquisitions of personal data.

In terms of the access interest, the Privacy Directive offers broad protection:

> 'Member States shall guarantee every data subject the right to obtain from the controller:
>
> — confirmation as to whether or not data relating to him are being processed . . .
>
> — communication to him in an intelligible form of the data undergoing processing . . .
>
> — as appropriate the rectification, erasure or blocking of data the processing of which does not comply with the provisions of this Directive.' (Article 12).

The access right is in itself positive for consumer confidence, but is qualified by the right of data processors to make a non-excessive charge for its exercise[69] (eg, in the UK the ceiling is GBP10—about 14 euros).[70] From a consumer point of view the charge is a disincentive to the exercise of the right and it might be argued that whilst the data processor takes the benefit of personal data, it should also take the reasonable burdens associated therewith and thus be obliged to provide free access on reasonable demand, ie where the demand is not vexacious. In an age of automated data processing it seems unlikely that this could be considered an unduly heavy burden on processors. At the least the Directive might have imposed a ceiling on a nominal charge.[71] Further, consumers currently have to pay even if they find that the data processor holds incorrect data. This seems unduly burdensome for the individual given that corrections of data are a service of value to the data processor.

It can further be argued that the Directive does not provide an effective remedial scheme. It does require Member States to offer consumers a judicial remedy where their privacy is breached[72] and to establish within their respective territories a supervisory authority,[73] with whom processors have to register.[74] However, mandating a bare judicial remedy does not adequately reflect the diffuse nature of consumers' privacy interest, a judicial remedy will often be unattractive to individual consumers given the typical costs of litigation on the one hand and the privacy benefit to be gained on the other. The Directive could have recognised the diffuse nature of privacy interests by providing for punitive

[69] Article 12(a).

[70] The Data Protection (Subject Access) (Fees) Regulations 1987 (SI 1987/1507).

[71] For example, the Directive could have set a figure, to increase in line with inflation, or provided for its amendment by Commission Decision.

[72] 'Member States shall provide for the right to every person to a judicial remedy for any breach of the rights guaranteed him by the national law applicable to the processing in question', (Article 22).

[73] Article 28.

[74] Article 18.

damages or private representative actions, or both; the former are well-established in Community competition law,[75] and the latter in Community consumer law.[76]

The Directive's deficiencies in ensuring redress are not limited to its provisions in respect of the Community itself, but extend also to transfers of data to third countries. Although the Directive does impose an obligation on Member States to ensure that transfers to unsafe third countries are not made (Article 25), it provides no effective remedy for the individual who is prejudiced by a breach of this rule. This is of particular concern given that many of the most popular commercial Web-sites are in the US, a country which accords a low priority to data protection (the Community's 'Safe Harbour' agreement with the US is discussed below). Community and national authorities will often be unable to take any effective action against third-country data processors to whom data are unlawfully transmitted by a controller within the Community.[77] The focus of the Directive seems to be the facilitation of trans-border data flows in the interests of data processors, rather than the protection of privacy (this might also be argued to be the case with the OECD Guidelines[78] and the Council of Europe Convention).[79]

Finally, the effectiveness of the Privacy Directive and the Directive on e-privacy has been hampered by slow transposition by the Member States. As regards the Privacy Directive, although all Member States have now implemented it, the process took many years, with only four Member States implementing on

[75] See Article 23(2) of Regulation 1/2003 empowering the Commission to fine a company 10% of its annual turnover where the latter engages in certain breaches of Article 81 or 82 EC. See generally: W Wils, 'Competition Fines: to Deter or not to Deter' [1995] *Yearbook of European Law* 17; M Polinsky and S Shavell, 'Punitive Damages: an Economic Analysis' (1998) 111 *Harvard Law Review* 861.

[76] For example, Article 7 of Directive 93/13/EC on unfair terms in consumer contracts provides for private consumer organisations to take legal action against such terms.

[77] See generally: Commission Working Party on the Protection of Individuals with regard to the Processing of Personal Data, *Transfers of personal data to third countries: Applying Articles 25 and 26 of the EU data protection directive* (Working Document DG XV D/5025/98, www.europa.eu.int/comm/internal_market/en/media/dataprot, July 1998).

[78] Page 117 above, Article 17: 'A Member country should refrain from restricting transborder flows of personal data between itself and another Member country except where the latter does not yet substantially observe these Guidelines or where the re-export of such data would circumvent its domestic privacy legislation.'

[79] Article 12(2) of Convention 108 for the Protection of Individuals with Regard to the Automatic Processing of Personal Data (1981) provides that 'a party shall not, for the sole purpose of the protection of privacy, prohibit or subject to special authorisation transborder flows of personal data going to the territory of another Party . . . except where the regulations of the other Party provide an equivalent protection . . . or . . . when the transfer is made from its territory to the territory of a non-contracting State through the intermediary of the territory of another Party, in order to avoid such transfers resulting in circumvention of the legislation of the Party referred to at the beginning of this paragraph.' The text of the Convention can be found at http://conventions.coe.int.

time.[80] As regards the Directive on e-privacy, the Commission in December 2003 launched infringement proceedings against nine Member States for failure properly to implement.[81]

Spam

> 'Where electronic contact details are obtained, the customer should be informed about their further use for direct marketing in a clear and distinct manner, and be given the opportunity to refuse such usage.' *Recital 41, Directive 2002/58 on e-privacy.*

The Community failed to deal explicitly with the problem of spam until 2002, although it would seem in fact to be illegal under the Privacy Directive of 1995: as explained above, the Privacy Directive broadly forbids the automatic processing of personal data without consent, which is precisely what is usually involved in sending spam. Strangely, this point seems never to have been pursued in the courts.

Prior to 2002, the Community passed up a number of opportunities to explicitly outlaw spam. The Directive on e-commerce of 2001 neither prohibits it nor makes it subject to prior consent, but merely provides that it must be clearly and unequivocally identifiable as spam as soon as it is received by the recipient.[82] The Directive on distance contracts of 1997 provides that Member States can choose between opt-in and opt-out schemes,[83] and the Telecoms Privacy Directive of the same year made similar provision.[84]

Finally, in 2002 the Community acted by adopting the Directive on e-privacy.[85] Electronic mail is therein defined broadly:

[80] See D Korff, 'Study on Implementation of Data Protection Directive—Comparative Summary of National laws' (www.europa.eu.int/comm/internal_market/en/media/dataprot, May 2003). Late transposition is a common failing of Community law, another more extreme example is that of Directive 94/47/EC on timeshares, which only two Member States managed to transpose on time (Commission, *Report on the Application of Directive 94/47/EC of the European Parliament and Council of 26 October 1994 on the protection of purchasers in respect of certain aspects of contracts relating to the purchase of the right to use immovable properties on a timeshare basis* (www.europa.eu.int/comm/dg24/policy/developments/timeshare/time02_en.html, 1999). See generally on the dependence of Community law on national enforcement mechanisms: F Snyder, 'The Effectiveness of European Community Law: Institutions, Processes, Tools and Techniques' (1992) 56 *Modern Law Review* 19.

[81] Press release IP/03/1663.

[82] Article 7.

[83] Article 10 (which does however prohibit the use of fax machines and automatic calling machines without the prior consent of the consumer).

[84] Article 12(2) of Directive 97/66/EC concerning the processing of personal data and the protection of privacy in the telecommunications sector, now replaced by Directive 2002/58 on e-privacy, note 58 above.

[85] Note 58 above.

'any text, voice, sound or image message sent over a public communications network which can be stored in the network or in the recipient's terminal equipment until it is collected by the recipient.' (Article 2(h)).

The essence of the concept is that of an electronic message not requiring the simultaneous presence of the sender and the recipient. The definition is broad and designed to be technology-neutral, including traditional 'Simple Mail Transport Protocol'-based email, Short Message Service-based mail (text messages), Multimedia Messaging Service-based mail, and voice messages left on answering machines.

Article 13(1) of the Directive provides the basic prohibition of spam:

'The use of automated calling systems without human intervention (automatic calling machines), facsimile machines (fax) or electronic mail for the purposes of direct marketing may only be allowed in respect of subscribers who have given their prior consent.'

The term consent is defined in Article 2(f) by reference to Article 2(h) of the Privacy Directive, which provides that the data subject's consent is 'any freely given specific and informed indication of his wishes by which the data subject signifies his agreement to personal data related to him being processed.' Recital 17 of the Directive on e-privacy goes on to re-affirm the need for positive action on the part of the data subject, indicating as an example of such action the specific ticking of a box on a website. The Article 29 Data Protection Working Party has gone on to state that pre-ticked boxes on websites cannot satisfy the requirement of 'informed indication'.[86]

Article 13 further provides for the obligation to offer an opt-out possibily each time a message is sent:

'. . . where a natural or legal person obtains from its customers their electronic contact details for electronic mail . . . the same . . . person may use these electronic contact details for direct marketing of its own similar products or services provided that customers clearly and distinctly are given the opportunity to object, free of charge and in an easy manner, to such use of electronic contact details when they are collected and on the occasion of each message in case the customer has not initially refused such use.' (Article 13(2)).

Whilst this obligation is in itself a positive step, it would have been better if it had provided that the opt-out possibility should be exercisable by the same method as that used to send the message. Similarly, it could have provided a time-limit for the validity of the consent—currently it is moot whether a producer can continue to send emails to customers five and ten years after consent was given. Finally, some further definition of 'similar products and services'

[86] Opinion 5/2004 on unsolicited communications for marketing purposes under Article 13 of Directive 2002/58/EC, www.europa.eu.int/comm/privacy.

would have been useful. From a consumer confidence perspective, this term would have been best defined by the reasonable expectations of the consumer.[87] It is certainly possible to see different perspectives—for example, a buyer of wood from a DIY shop might be surprised to receive marketing for stair-lifts for the disabled whilst the shop might argue that both products are similar because both are for the home.

It is positive that the Community acted in 2002 explicitly to prohibit spam. However, its slow response can be criticised, and contrasted with the stricter stances taken by various States in the US, most of which have legislated to combat spam.[88] Common features of these statutes are that they:—prohibit the forging of addresses and routing information, require opt-out instructions to be included and honoured, prohibit the use of misleading subject-line headers. Some require indication of the nature of the message in the header, eg through use of 'ADV', or 'ADV:ADULT' in the case of adult-oriented material. The penalties are generally based on fines per unsolicited e-mail sent, typically ten dollars with a maximum of 25,000 dollars per day.[89] Exceptionally, criminal penalties are attached, for example in California imprisonment for up to three years,[90] and in Virginia for up to five years.[91] A final comparison is that of Germany, where spam has long been prohibited by the civil law.[92]

Co-ordination

> '. . . as the volume of transborder flow increases, the control possibilities diminish. It becomes much more difficult, for example, to identify the countries through which data will transit before reaching the authorised recipient. Problems of data security and confidentiality are heightened when data are piped through communication lines which traverse countries where little or no attention is accorded to issues of data protection.
>
> In brief, when advanced communication networks enable businessmen on foreign travels to access their enterprises' data bases via hand-held computers plugged into sockets available in airports and to down-load data instantaneously into their

[87] Supported by Opinion 5/2004, note 86 above, at 9.

[88] See D Sorkin, www.spamlaws.com (also Congress adopted the federal CAN-SPAM Act in 2003).

[89] Virginia, Rhode Island, and Illinois all adopt that scheme, see Sorkin, note 88 above.

[90] See California Penal Code, s502.

[91] Virginia Code, s18.2–152.

[92] Information and Communications Law Act 1997, per P Rott, 'The Distance Selling Directive and German Law', in B Stauder (ed), *Protection des Consommateurs Acheteurs à Distance* (Brussels, Schultess/Bruylant, 1999).

computers across vast distances, the issue of national regulation of transborder data flows becomes problematic indeed.' (Council of Europe, 1989).[93]

The Community has further engaged in *co-ordinating* laws, attempting to ensure that privacy rights are enforceable across national borders within and outside the Community. Within the Community, the Brussels Regulation of 2000[94] provides that a person domiciled in one Member States may, in another Member State, be sued in matters relating to tort, delict or quasi-delict in the courts for the place where the harmful event occurred or may occur (Article 5(3)). Although it is not clear how this provision applies to privacy, in the case of *Mines de Potasse*,[95] the European Court of Justice held that those suffering damage pursuant to the release by a mine of toxins into a river could sue either in the country in which the damage was suffered, or in the country in which the mine was situated. Similarly, in the case of *Shevill*[96] the Court held that defamatory statements within a newspaper circulated in several jurisdictions gave rise to a right on the part of the defamed person to choose whether to sue in the jurisdiction of the defendant's domicile, for all damage caused, or in individual jurisidictions, for the damage in the relevant jurisdiction or jurisdictions. An action for a typical cross-border breach of privacy (eg a Web-site in Member State X collecting personal data without consent from a consumer in Member State Y) can be analogised to both of these cases as the act causing the damage and the damage itself can be conceptualised as taking place in different locations. Thus it can be argued that in such cases consumers can sue for breach of their privacy either in their country of domicile or in the country in which the data processor is domiciled. However, although a right of action exists, no case has been reported and indeed litigation seems unlikely given the probable cost, which highlights the importance of the point made above about the need for more accessible remedies.

Rules as regards applicable law have not been harmonised, although the Commission in 2002 published a Proposal for a Regulation on the law applicable to non-contractual obligations ('Rome II').[97] The general rule proposed

[93] *New Technologies: A Challenge to Privacy Protection?* (1989) at para 6.9. Although once active in the field of privacy, the Council of Europe would appear to have ceded its responsibilities to the Community, see the 1981 Convention 108 for the Protection of Individuals with Regard to the Automatic Processing of Personal Data Strasbourg, (www.coe.int). The Convention was a creation of nation-states; it was and is non-binding, although it inspired a number of national laws, for example the Data Protection Act 1984 in the UK, detailed, but not reproduced, at www.open.gov.uk/dpr/dprhome.htm. The Council of Europe was active in the field throughout 1980s, adopting a series of sector-specific recommendations, the last one coming in 1991 (Recommendation (91)10, Protection of Personal Data Used for Payment and Other Related Operations).

[94] Chapter 2 note 107 above.

[95] Case 21/76 *Handelskwekerij GJ Bier v Mines de Potasse d'Alsace* [1976] ECR 1753.

[96] Case C–68/93 *Shevill v Presse Alliance* [1995] ECR I–415.

[97] COM(2003) 427.

is that the applicable law be the law of the country in which the damage arises or is likely to arise, irrespective of the country in which the event giving rise to the damage occurred (Article 3(1)). Where the application of such law in the context of a non-contractual obligation arising out of a violation of privacy or rights relating to the personality would be contrary to the fundamental principles of the forum as regards freedom of expression and information then the law applicable shall be that of the forum (Article 6C1)).

Consumers are less well-protected as regards the processing of their data outside the Community than they are within the Community. Although agreements have been struck with third countries within the scope of Article 25 of the Privacy Directive,[98] those agreements reflect the flaws of the Directive itself—the agreement with most importance for consumers being that with the US[99] and this is considered in detail below.

US 'Safe Harbour'

The United States has traditionally taken the view that the right to privacy is best guarded by individuals themselves, who are generally free in private relations to disclose or not to disclose their data, and further that public regulation of private data processing is an unacceptable restriction on the right to free speech.[100] The former point would seem to be something of a fiction in modern times—standard-form contracts often demand that consumers hand over their personal data and control thereof. In fields of commerce with a limited number of operators, it would seem that consumers often have little choice but to agree to hand over control of their data if they want the good or service in question, which will in some cases be one which they cannot realistically do without. Yet the hold of the right to free speech on the American psyche is powerful, and although a variety of controls on data processing have been suggested, including granting individuals property in their personal information,[101] and forbidding the buying or selling of personal data,[102] the legal system has not taken up these suggestions.

[98] Page 127 above.

[99] It is the most important given the large number of online sellers based there.

[100] It should not however be thought that the US and EU systems have nothing in common, the study by the Federal Trade Commission 1998, note 23 above, surveyed existing privacy protection in the United States, Canada and Europe and found the following common principles (subject of course to the countervailing right of free speech): 1 notice 2 consent 3 access 4 security 5 enforcement/redress, at 7–11.

[101] C Shapiro and H Varian, *US Government Information Policy* (www.sims.berkeley.edu/~hal/papers/policy/policy.htm, 1998).

[102] J Litman, 'Information Privacy/Information Property' (1999) 52 *Stanford Law Review* 1 at 20, analogising data to entities which cannot be owned such as navigable waterways, people, human rights), and the use of tort law (*ibid.*).

The courts have struck down a number of federal efforts to regulate data protection as infringements of the right to free speech.[103] The limited statutory protection which the US does provide is generally applicable only to the activities of public bodies, the rationale for this being that individuals are not free to withhold particular data from public bodies. The principal relevant statute is the Privacy Act of 1974, requiring governmental organisations creating personal data files to do so only as far as is necessary for the particular purpose in question, to inform the subject, to take reasonable care to ensure that the files are accurate and are kept secure. The only statute generally applicable to private entities is the Video Privacy Protection Act 1988,[104] which protects data relating to the videos an individual hires or buys (it is odd that the United States should regard this data as worthy of protection, but not medical information!). In addition to these statutes, the common-law provides some privacy protections,[105] but these have not been broadly developed by the courts. Commentators have suggested various cultural explanations of the US approach—trust in the power of the market, media and technology, as well as a strong tradition of protecting free speech.[106]

This contrast with the EU position gave rise in 1995 to negotiations over how the privacy of EU citizens might be protected in the US (doubtless US concern was partly driven by a desire to ensure that the EU did not use the issue as a justification for excluding US businesses from the European marketplace).[107] These negotiations took place within the framework of Article 25 of the Privacy Directive:

> 'The transfer to a third country of data which are undergoing processing or which are intended for processing shall take place only if . . . the third country ensures an adequate level of protection. The adequacy of the level of protection afforded by a

[103] For example: *US West v FCC*, 182 F.3d 1224 (10th Cir 1999); *Pryor v Reno* 171 F.3d 1281 (11th Cir 1999).

[104] 18 USC section 2710–11 (1994).

[105] See eg Section 625B of the Restatement (Second) of Torts: 'one who intentionally intrudes, physically or otherwise, upon the solitude or seclusion of another or his private affairs or concerns, is subject to liability to the other for invasion of his privacy, if the intrusion would be highly offensive to a reasonable person'.

[106] R Litan and P Swire, *None of your Business: World Data Flows, Electronic Commerce, and the European Privacy Directive* (Washington DC, Brookings Institution Press, 1998) at 7 and following, and (specifically discussing the role of the First Amendment in protecting freedom of speech) at 153. See also: J Kang, 'Information Privacy in Cyberspace Transactions' (1998) 50 *Stan L Rev* 1193; S Garfinkel, *Database Nation: The Death of Privacy in the 21st Century* (New York, O'Reilly & Associates, 2000); J Reidenberg and P Schwartz, *Data Protection Law and On-line Services: Regulatory Responses* (www.europa.eu.int/comm/internal_market/en/media/dataprot, 1999); L Brandeis and S Warren, 'The Right to Privacy' (1890) 4 *Harvard Law Review* 193.

[107] See generally, G Shaffer, 'The Power of EU Collective Action: The Impact of EU Data Privacy Regulation on US Business Practices' (1999) 5 *European Law Journal*, www.iue.it/law/ELJ; R Lowther, 'US Privacy Regulations Dictated by EU Law: How the Healthcare Profession may be Regulated' 41 (2003) *Columbia Journal of Transnational Law* 435.

third country shall be assessed in the light of all the circumstances surrounding a data transfer operation or set of data transfer operations; particular consideration shall be given to the nature of the data, the purpose and duration of the proposed processing operation or operations, the country of origin and country of final destination, the rules of law both general and sectoral, in force in the third country in question and the professional rules and security measures which are complied with in that country.'

The negotiations between the US and the Commission in relation to Article 25 were attended by a lack of clarity which echoes that of the Privacy Directive discussed above.[108] Certain Commission documents relating to the negotiations were available to the European public only through the US Department of Commerce; these documents included a draft Commission decision on the 'adequacy' of US data protection standards within the meaning of Article 25 of the Directive.[109] Whilst the European Parliament was able to play no more than an advisory role in those negotiations,[110] it is difficult to see why Article 26 procedures were not made not subject to the co-decision procedure,[111] which might now be argued to be the accepted standard in EU law-making.[112] (The Community, or at least the Parliament, would seem to have learnt from the mistakes of the Privacy Directive—provisions giving to the Commission the power to decide on the compatibility with Community law of national derogations from a general right freely to provide information society services anywhere in the Community were included in a draft of the Directive on e-commerce, but omitted from the final version.)[113]

The first set of negotiations between the US and EU ended in July 2000, with agreement being reached on a system of 'Safe Harbor' Principles to govern the holding of EU citizens' personal data by US businesses.[114] The Principles are summarised below:

108 Page 119 above.

109 *Per* Bureau Europeen de Consommateurs, *BEUC in Brief* (www.beuc.org, December 1999) at 5. The Department of Commerce Web site is at www.ita.doc.gov/.

110 Articles 25 and 31 of the Privacy Directive provide for decision by the Commission acting in concert with the Council. See the Report of the Committee on Citizens' Freedoms and Rights, Justice and Home Affairs on the Draft Commission Decision on the adequacy of the protection provided by the Safe Harbour Privacy Principles (C5–0280/2000–2000 –200/2144(COS), (The 'Paciotti Report'), http://www.europarl.eu.int/plenary/en/default.htm#reports. Parliament's objections were over-ridden by the Commission.

111 Article 251 EC.

112 C Crombez, 'Co-decision: Towards a Bicameral European Union' (2000) 1 *European Union Politics* 363.

113 See Commission, *Proposal for a Directive on e-commerce*, COM(98) 586, Articles 22 and 23. The Commission was to have been assisted by an Advisory Committee made up of representatives from Member States' governments.

114 See Commission Decision C(2000) 2441: (http://europa.eu.int/comm/internal_market/en/media/dataprot/news/decision.pdf, 2000). The Principles and related FAQ can be found at: http://europa.eu.int/comm/internal_market/en/media/dataprot/news/safeharbor.htm, and at: http://www.export.gov/safeharbor/sh_documents.htm.

1 **Notice:** an organisation must inform individuals about the purposes for which it collects and uses information about them, how to contact the organisation with any queries or complaints, the types of third parties to which it discloses the information, and the choices and means offered for limiting its use.
2 **Choice:** individuals must be offered the opportunity to choose whether their personal information is to be disclosed to a third party or to be used for a purpose incompatible with the purpose for which it was originally collected (ie an opt-out).
3 **Onward transfer:** where individuals have been notified of and consented to the possibility of a transfer to a third party, such transfer may take place where the third party subscribes to the Safe Harbour Principles or enters into a written agreement with the transferor promising that the third party will provide at least the same level of privacy protection as is required by the Safe Harbour Principles.
4 **Security:** processors must take reasonable precautions to protect personal data from loss, misuse and unauthorised access, disclosure, alteration and destruction.
5 **Data Integrity:** an organisation may not process personal data in a way that is incompatible with the purposes for which it has been collected or subsequently authorised by the individual.
6 **Access:** individuals must have access to personal information about them that an organisation holds and be able to correct, amend, or delete that information where it is inaccurate, except where the burden or expense of providing access would be disproportionate to the risks to the individual's privacy in the case in question, or where the rights of persons other than the individual would be violated.
7 **Enforcement:** organisations must put in place mechanisms for assuring compliance, as well as readily available and affordable recourse for individuals who are affected by non-compliance (including damages where the applicable law or private sector initiatives so provide).[115]

Organisations self-certify compliance with the Principles to the Federal Trade Commission, and once done, companies within Europe can freely transfer personal data to them.[116]

Although the Principles appear broadly to satisfy consumers' privacy interests, there exist a number of gaps. First, the Principles allow the collection of personal data without notice—the Notice Principle above provides that notice can occur 'as soon after collection as is practicable'. The Principles do not provide consumers with the right to have data collected in this way deleted. This does not satisfy consumers' interest in consent.

[115] The Principles do not affect questions of jurisdiction and choice of law: *per* letter of 27 July 2000 from the Director-General for the Internal Market to the Under-Secretary for Trade in the US Department of Commerce: 'I would like to confirm that it is the Commission's intention that participation in the 'safe harbor' does not change the status quo ante for any organisation with respect to jurisdiction, applicable law or liability in the European Union. Moreover, our discussions with respect to the 'safe harbor' have not resolved nor prejudged the questions of jurisdiction or applicable law with respect to websites', letter available at http://www.ita.doc.gov/td/ecom/EUletter27JulyHeader.htm.

[116] FAQ, note 114 above, No. 7.

Second, where access to data would impose disproportionate 'burden or expense' on the seller, it can be denied.[117] This condition is vague and does not satisfy consumers' interest in access. It contrasts sharply with the Directive, which allows sellers to restrict access only in tightly-controlled circumstances.[118]

Third, consumers have no remedy against a processor transferring their personal data to a third party who signs an agreement to protect the data—as long as the transferor complies with the requirement to obtain a written agreement, then:

> 'it shall not be held responsible . . . when a third party to which it transfers such information processes it in a way contrary to any restrictions or representations, unless the organization knew or should have known the third party would process it in such a contrary way and the organization has not taken reasonable steps to prevent or stop such processing.'[119]

Thus if the third party reneges on the agreement, it would seem that the consumer will be without a remedy. Certainly the transferor will have little incentive in bringing an action for breach of contract, given that its own loss will be minimal or nil.

Fourth, in the event of a consumer having a legitimate complaint against a particular processor, it is not clear what rights he has to ensure that the problem is resolved. Under the 'Enforcement Principle' the processor in question must inform him of the ADR body to which he can complain, but if that avenue proves fruitless, he would appear to be without a remedy. Whilst the Federal Trade Commission has general powers to impose sanctions on processors for unfair and deceptive trade practices (under section 5 of the Federal Trade Commission Act), it has no duty to deal with individual complaints.[120]

Fifth, the Principles suffer from dubious democratic legitimacy. The Decision was taken in the teeth of objections—centring around those detailed above—from the European Parliament.[121]

To conclude, Safe Harbour can be seen as a replica of the domestic US system which has, according to the FTC, failed to protect US citizens' privacy online.[122] The Principles may be better for EU citizens than the absence of any

[117] FAQ, note 114 above, no. 8(1) and (2). This would also seem to extend to the protection of commercially sensitive information.

[118] Access can only be restricted where necessary for the rights and freedoms of others (Article 13). (Of course this only applies to private data processors, other exceptions do exist for public processors, for reasons of national security etc.).

[119] Onward Transfer Principle.

[120] FAQ, note 114 above, no. 11.

[121] See Report of the Committee on Citizens' Freedoms and Rights, Justice and Home Affairs, A5–0177/2000, PE 285.929/DEF.

[122] This is the general thrust of FTC 2000, note 12 above.

agreement,[123] but they leave gaps which only more intensive co-operation would seem able to fill.

The final aspect of the EU-US relationship to be noted is that of the transfer of air passenger name records to the United States public authorities. In May 2004 the Council and the Commission published controversial decisions on the same.[124] The Decisions are unclear as to scope of the data to be retained, the retention period and the way in which they are to be used,[125] and the European Parliament has taken the issue to the European Court of Justice.[126]

Observations

Although the Community has instituted a broad public law framework to protect consumers' privacy, there are serious gaps in that framework in the context of the Internet. The Directives in question neither ensure that data is only collected with consumers' consent (ie there is no provision for conspicuous notice or opt-in) nor do they institute a private remedial framework appropriate for the diffuse nature of the privacy interest. Furthermore, parts of the Privacy Directive are unclear, and its application to processors in the United States through the Safe Harbour Principles leaves consumers with significantly less protection than they have in Europe. Finally, only a minority of Member States implemented the Directives on time.

In order to generate confidence, the Community's data protection framework must be made effective for individuals at a global level, ie it must reflect the reality of the marketplace itself, and this cannot be said to be the case at the moment, particularly with regard to the Safe Harbour Principles. Paradoxically, if the Community can provide such a framework, it may concomitantly strengthen self-regulatory mechanisms. In particular, the educative value of legal norms and the existence of binding sanctions may encourage businesses to take a greater interest in *effective* trustmarks which can attract knowledgeable data subjects.[127]

Having considered the Community's protection of consumers' fair trading and privacy interests, attention will now be turned to the field of consumers' moral interests.

[123] Even this is not guaranteed. The existence of the Safe Harbour principles may distract attention from the fact that EU citizens' privacy is not being protected in the US and may delay the introduction of a protective system while they are given 'time to work'.

[124] Council Decision 2004/496/EC, Commission Decision 2004/535/EC.

[125] See Article 29 Working Party Report of 22 June 2004.

[126] Case C–317/04.

[127] Schwartz, note 48 above, at 1697.

4

Consumers III—Moral Interests

Threats to Consumers' Moral Interests

> 'Four out of ten children have who have chatted on the Internet say that people they have only met on the Net have asked to meet them in person.' *European Commission, Proposal for a Decision establishing a programme on promoting safer use of the Internet.*[1]

Chapter 1 identified consumers' critical moral interests in e-commerce as those concerning the need to protect children from explicitly sexual and violent online material, and to a lesser extent (in quantitative terms), the need to protect them from sexual predators in (commercially-provided) chat-rooms. The threats to those interests within the electronic marketplace are driven by the Internet's powerful and undiscriminating ability to disseminate speech coupled in some cases with the ability to support anonymity.[2] Larry Lessig has pointed out the link between the US origins of the Net and how its architecture supports US-style free speech: 'we have exported to the world, through the architecture of the Internet, a First Amendment in code more extreme than our own First Amendment in law'.[3] As the US Supreme Court has noted:

> 'Through the use of chat rooms, any person with a phone line can become a town crier with a voice that resonates further than it could from any soapbox. Through

[1] COM(2004) 91 at 3.

[2] As discussed in chapter 1 above. See in particular the case of *Zeran v AOL* (1997) 129 F 3d 327, US Ct of Apps (4th Cir).

[3] *Code and Other Laws of Cyberspace* (New York, Basic Books, 1999) at 167.

the use of Web pages, mail exploders, and newsgroups, the same individual can become a pamphleteer . . .' US Supreme Court, *ACLU v Reno*.[4]

It is impossible to quantify with any precision the problem of harmful Internet content, whether in terms of the amount of content, the extent to which it is accessed, or the harm it causes. However, it is clear that computer use amongst children is very common—one recent survey covering Denmark, Ireland, Sweden, Norway and Iceland found that 97 per cent of children aged 9 to 16 years had used a computer.[5] Furthermore, surveys have long found large quantities of explicit sexual material on the Net—one 1995 article noted that the most popular newsgroup in the world by traffic volume was alt.binaries.pictures.erotica, and that 'pedophilic [material] . . . is widely available through various computer networks and protocols'.[6] The site *searchterms.com* as at August 2000 (the site late became defunct and the searchterm rankings at the more popular search engines exclude sex-related terms) listed 'sex' as the third most popular search term and fourteen of the top fifty search terms were sex-related, namely: free porn (14), porn (19), free sex (24), free sex pics (31), xxx (32), lolita (35), pussy (37), porno (39), playboy (43), free sex pictures (46), hentai [animated erotica] (49), erotic stories (50).[7]

There are significant dangers of accidental access by children to sexually-explicit material. Searches related to various interests of children—including 'Bambi', 'Sleeping Beauty', 'Minnie', 'girls', 'boys', 'dolls', 'toys'—have all been reported as returning sex-related sites.[8] Opening the site 'whitehouse.com' rather than 'whitehouse.gov' brings up pornography rather than the White House of the United States President.

In addition to the dangers of accidental access, children may actively seek and find adult material—the most obvious site for a child curious about sex is http://www.sex.com, and as at March 2004 the home-page of this site contained explicit, animated sexual material. It had no warning that it was unsuitable for children and attempts to leave the site resulted in the user being

[4] 929 F. Supp. 830, (www.aclu.org/court/cdadec.html), (judgement of special 3-judge panel).

[5] *Proposal for a Decision of the European Parliament and of the Council on establishing a multi-annual Community programme on promoting safer use of the Internet and new online technologies*, COM(2004) 91 at 3.

[6] M Rimm, 'Marketing Pornography on the Information Superhighway: A Survey of 917,410 Images, Descriptions, Short Stories, and Animations Downloaded 8.5 Million Times by Consumers in over 2,000 Cities in Forty Countries, Provinces and Territories' (1995) 83 *Georgetown University Law Journal* 1849 at 1914.

[7] In 1997 the New York Times reported that 8% of online consumers of pornography are teenagers: A Harmon, 'For Parents a New and Vexing Burden' (27 June 1997) at A21. Regarding online pornography generally see Y Akdeniz, *Sex on the Net* (Reading, South Street Press, 1999).

[8] See H Miller, 'Strike Two: An Analysis of the Child Online Protection Act's Constitutional Failures' (1999) 52 *Federal Communications Law Journal* 155 at 161.

'bounced' to other sex-related sites (bouncing occurred whether the attempt to leave the site was to another site or to close Netscape).[9] Word-searches related to sex, in any language, return large numbers of sexually-explicit sites. A recent study found that 44 per cent of children who use the Internet have visited a pornographic site by accident or on purpose.[10]

Web-sites may target children with inappropriate material, whether for commercial or other reasons, and ratings organisations have expressed the fear that material will in bad faith be self-rated as 'safe' for children.[11] Targeting via Web-sites can be achieved by inserting words which reflect children's interests into Web-page metatags—relevant searches for those words will then find those Web-sites.

Hate-speech (including violent material) is not as prevalent online as sexually-explicit material, no doubt because it does not have the same revenue-generating capacity. Thus the possibilities of accidentally coming across such material are much less. However the problem of curious children looking for it remains—the Commission's *Proposal for a Decision on promoting safer use of the Internet* of 2004 reported that 30 per cent of children have seen Web-sites with violent material, although only 15 per cent of parents think their children have done so.[12] Overt race-hate material is openly available online.[13] A search for the word 'Nazi' returned a number of hate-speech sites, including that of the American Nazi Party.[14] A further particular problem is that children may search for, and find, material related to violent films. A search carried out by this author in March 2004 via *Google* for one such film, 'The Shining', found many thousands of related sites. *Google* did not show any warning that these sites might contain violent material. The same was true of *Yahoo!*'s listings under 'horror film sites'.

As with explicitly sexual and violent online material, the problem of paedophiles using chat-rooms to contact children is difficult to quantify. However, the Commission's 2004 *Proposal for a Decision on promoting safer use of the Internet* reports that 14 per cent of children have met someone in person whom they first met online (only 4 per cent of parents think they have done this).[15]

[9] Such 'bouncing' can be countered by pressing the CTRL and W keys simultaneously, or by shutting down windows as soon as they open.

[10] COM(2004) 91 at 3.

[11] See eg http://www.safesurf.com/ssfaq.htm#selfrate, (the role of ratings organisations in protecting children is discussed below).

[12] COM(2004) 91 at 3.

[13] See eg http://members.aol.com/poloboy02/nazi1.htm. See generally, Institute for Jewish Policy Research, 'The governance of cyberspace: racism on the Internet' (http://www1.us.nizkor.com/ftp.cgi/orgs/british/jewish-policy-research/internet-regulation.9609, 1996).

[14] www.americannaziparty.com.

[15] Note 12 above, at 3.

The following section will address the extent to which self-help can neutralise these threats.

Self-help as a Solution?

> 'Practical measures are still needed . . . to encourage development of filtering technologies, to spread best practice for codes of conduct embodying generally agreed canons of behaviour, and to inform and educate parents and children on the best way to benefit from the potential of new media in a safe way.' *European Commission, Proposal for a Decision establishing a programme on promoting safer use of the Internet.*[16]

A number of commentators have expressed the view that self-help is capable of generating confidence in content amongst users.[17] In a tone which has long been taken by those who celebrate the Net's ability to loosen the censor's shackles, the content-rating organisation Safesurf has stated,

> 'The Internet community has long required proper 'netiquette' of its members, and has been very effective in enforcing this netiquette. We believe abusers will be shut down in a nanosecond by this structure. We believe in the power of the Net. Our system will demonstrate that cooperative self-help is a million times more effective that governmental censorship.'[18]

Children's non-use and supervised-use of the Internet might be considered the first avenues of parental self-help. However, these avenues can be considered ineffective given the fact that Internet access is available in many libraries, homes, schools and as part of mobile phone services. In the light of such easy access to the Internet it is difficult for parents adequately to control their children's use of it. (The potential of software to act as a 'proxy supervisor' is considered below).

A second avenue of self-help can be identified as the 'hotlines' which consumers can use to report harmful content to ISPs and law enforcement authorities (hotlines can be considered a hybrid of self-help and public regulation). Consumers may often be more willing to report harmful content to a hotline than to make a formal complaint to the police. A good example of a successful hotline is that run by the Internet Watch Foundation ('IWF') in the UK.[19] The

[16] Note 12 above, at 11.

[17] See eg Center for Democracy and Technology, 'Internet Family Empowerment White Paper' (www.cdt.org/speech/empower.html/, July 1997); E Dyson, *Release 2.1 A Design for living in the digital age* (New York, Broadway Books, 1998) at 212–14.

[18] http://www.safesurf.com/ssfaq.htm#selfrate, at 14 July 2003. The role of Safesurf is considered further below.

[19] www.iwf.org.uk.

IWF receives complaints via telephone, fax, and the Internet, passes them onto law enforcement bodies and ISPs, both domestic and foreign, and collates information as to subsequent action. The IWF has proved effective against illegal domestic content in the UK,[20] but, like other hotlines, it has generally proved powerless against foreign content-providers.[21] Further, ISPs may not be willing to remove material which is merely harmful, rather than illegal.

The third avenue of self-help in relation to online content is the filter, which can be used at ISP level or at the level of the consumer's computer. Examples of the use of filters at ISP-level include *Kidznet*,[22] which since 1997 has provided a service designed to give access only to sites which have been checked by employees.

Examples of consumer-level filters include CyberPatrol, KinderGuard, and SurfWatch.[23] These products use variously four techniques to protect children: negative lists of unsuitable sites; positive lists; searching incoming content for prohibited words (and sometimes by quantity of skin tone); and finally content ratings (discussed further below).

Both ISP- and consumer-level filters can make *rated* content inaccessible through installation of the Platform for Internet Content Selection ('PICS').[24] PICS is an Internet Protocol developed by the World Wide Web Consortium (an industry body established in 1994 to develop open standards for the Web);[25] it allows the content-provider, or some third party, to attach ratings to content under variable criteria, such as the nature of the content itself (violence/nudity/sex) and its context (art/medical/erotica). It is supported by standard browsers,[26] and has been hailed by many as the answer to obscene and child-unfriendly material on the Net.[27] An example of a PICS-compliant rating system is Safesurf,[28] in which material can be rated under nine categories:

[20] Per Y Akdeniz and C Walker, 'The Governance of the Internet in Europe with Special Reference to Illegal and Harmful Content', in C Walker (ed), *Criminal Law Review special edition: Crime, Criminal Justice and the Internet* (1998) at 14.

[21] *Ibid.*

[22] www.kidz.net.

[23] See eg www.surfwatch.org/about. A useful survey of these filters is provided in Internet Watch Foundation, *Self-labelling and Filtering* (www.ispo.cec.be/iap/decision/en.html, 2000).

[24] See generally: P Resnick, 'PICS-Interest@w3.org', http://lists.w3.org/archives/public/pics-interest/1999Jan/0000.html; 'PICS and intellectual freedom', http://www.w3.org/PICS/PICS-FAQ-980126.html.

[25] www.w3.org.

[26] See eg http://home.netscape.com/comprod/products/communicator/netwatch/.

[27] See eg Dyson, note 17 above, at 212–14.

[28] The Safesurf system is one of two recognised by Netscape, the other is that of the Internet Content Rating Association (an independent non-profit organisation—see www.icra.org).

— heterosexuality
— homosexuality
— profanity
— nudity
— violence
— intolerance
— glorifying drug use
— other adult themes
— gambling.[29]

Within each category there are nine levels: as an example, the full list for 'violence' is:

> 1 Subtle Innuendo, 2 Explicit Innuendo, 3 Technical Reference, 4 Non-Graphic-Artistic, 5 Graphic-Artistic, 6 Graphic, 7 Detailed Graphic, 8 Inviting Participation in Graphic Interactive Format, 9 Encouraging Personal Participation, Weapon Making.

Parents and others can set preferences within their PICS-enabled filter and only content which meets those preferences will be allowed through.

PICS clearly has some potential in enabling parents to protect their children online. *Safesurf*'s categories, for example, enable parents to screen out varying ranges of unsuitable material and may in that sense generate more confidence in online content than in content received through traditional media such as television, which parents can generally only filter by the cruder method of barring access. Many of the Web-sites which are attractive to children are likely to rate themselves, either because they are responsible information-providers, or because they have a commercial interest in doing so. Ratings organisations do check for inaccurate rating.[30] Although rating systems seem heavily focused on the English language,[31] PICS itself is not dependent on the use of any particular language on the part of the individual *consumer*.

Although filters have been shown to be generally effective at shielding children from undesirable content, they have also been shown to be restrictive in not allowing access to many educational sites of potential benefit to children (although some filters do alert users to the fact that a site has been blocked; thus children may ask a parent to override blocking in given cases).[32] It has been asserted that the ability to filter surreptitiously is insidious,[33] yet this

[29] www.safesurf.com. The ICRA system, note 28 above, is similar, although it uses only five categories (1 violence, 2 nudity and sex, 3 language, 4 chat, 5 other topics).

[30] For example, the ICRA system is protected by spot-checks of ratings, by Web-crawling for its logo, and by complaints, see www.icra.org.

[31] The ICRA site noted above also functions in German, French, Spanish and Italian.

[32] 'Internet Filters' (May 2000) *Which?* 38 at 38.

[33] See J Weinberg, 'Rating the Net' (1997) 19 *Hastings Communication and Entertainment Law Journal* 453, (www.law.wayne.edu/weinberg/rating.htm), citing disapprovingly at 461 that *Cybersitter* filters out feminist discussion groups.

form of filtering seems no more insidious than the filtering decisions taken by any other private media.

Notwithstanding the positive aspect of filters noted above, four criticisms can be made of them. First, they do not shut off access to all offensive material—it is almost inevitable that some will escape the controls.[34] Second, not all parents can afford them or have the technical expertise to install them.[35] Third, although the sophistication and flexibility of PICS is impressive, very few content-providers currently use it—the Internet Watch Foundation Report of 2000[36] concluded that sites rated in languages other than English are 'virtually non-existent', and that, 'the numbers [of English language sites] . . . still fall short of the "critical mass" required to persuade consumers to use [PICS-enabled filters]'.[37] It would seem unlikely that PICS will be taken up by a large proportion of content-providers given that they generally have no incentive to do so. Fourth, as noted above, filters often cut off some generally inoffensive sites and this can adversely affect consumers' general interest in having access to those sites.

One method of self-help which has not yet appeared, but which would appear to be potentially effective, is that which could be exercised by ICANN through its control of the Domain Name System root server.[38] As will be seen in chapter 6 below, the choke-point of the DNS root has proved valuable in preventing abuse of producers' interest in domain-name identity (in essence a trademark-based interest). In the field of consumers' morality interests online, ICANN could for example act against those adult sites indiscriminately displaying sexually explicit material—in effect pushing those sites into implementing age-related restrictions. Any move by ICANN to use the DNS root to control adult-oriented speech might well be controversial, but not necessarily any more controversial than its actions to control the use of trademarks in domain names, discussed in chapter 6 below. Both types of control are in essence restrictions on speech. Initially, age-related restrictions might simply be a requirement for users to state their age before being able to view explicit images—easily circumventable but such a restriction would at least protect children from accidentally coming across explicit home-pages.

In the light of ICANN's failure to act in the above and its speed in acting to protect trademark interests, a parallel might be drawn between the EU's focus on producers' interests in e-commerce identified in this book, and a similar

[34] Akdeniz and Walker, note 20 above, at 15 and following.

[35] The Internet Watch Foundation Report, note 57, Chapter 1 above, found that, 'most consumers would require some assistance to handle more complex filtering capabilities', at 30.

[36] Note 35 above.

[37] At 31 and 4. The Safesurf and ICRA sites at July 2003 reported no figures on how many sites have applied their rating systems, which can perhaps be regarded as an indicator that the numbers are low.

[38] See http://www.icann.org/committees/dns-root/.

focus within ICANN. The current dominance of (the US-based) ICANN in controlling the infrastructure of the Internet has led the United Nations to instigate an inquiry into whether the UN itself should take over such control.[39]

To conclude this section, self-help in relation to controlling harmful online content has only a limited role to play in screening out the most obviously unsuitable sites for those who have the requisite money and technical expertise. It is otherwise restricted in its ability to protect consumers' moral interests in e-commerce, in particular within the many households unable to afford filters. The following section analyses the extent to which the Community fills this gap.

Community Regulation

Supporting Self-help

Explicit Community support for self-help in relation to harmful online content first appeared in the Commission's *Communication on Restricting Access to Illegal and Harmful Content on the Internet* (1996),[40] which recommended that Internet Service Providers require site-providers to rate their own content. The European Parliament joined the fray shortly afterwards, asserting that illegal content would be easier to regulate than harmful content and that global action was the ideal.[41] The Council followed in 1999 with its *Decision on a multi-annual action plan on promoting safer use of the Internet.*[42] The Preamble to the Decision explicitly recognised the transnational nature of the problems dealt with therein:

> 'in conformity with the principle of subsidiarity as expressed in Article 3b of the Treaty, the objectives of the proposed actions cannot be sufficiently achieved by the Member States owing to the transnational character of the issues at stake and can,

[39] ICANN has pointed out in its defence that it moves more speedily in adopting new communications standards than the UN's International Telecommunications Union—6 months compared to two and a half years, *Financial Times* 25/3/04 at 11. See generally: A Murray, 'Regulation and Rights in Networked Space' (2003) 30(2) *Journal of Law & Society* 187.

[40] COM(96) 487.

[41] European Parliament, *Resolution on the Commission communication on illegal and harmful content on the Internet* (C4–0592/96).

[42] See www.europa.eu.int/comm/information_society/. See also Commission, *An action plan on promoting safe use of the Internet* (COM(97) 582) and Council Recommendation 98/560 on the development of the competitiveness of the European audio-visual and information services industry by promoting national frameworks aimed at achieving a comparable and effective level of protection of minors and human dignity (and Commission Reports thereon—COM(2001) 106, COM(2003) 776).

therefore, by reason of the pan-European effects of the proposed action be better achieved by the Community . . .' (Recital 21).

The Decision was based on the Community's competence in consumer protection,[43] and established an Action Plan running from 1999 until the end of 2002 (now extended to 2004, as discussed below), aimed at:

— building on industry hotline initiatives, and ensuring effective lines of communication between law enforcement authorities across the Member States,
— developing Codes of Conduct and quality labels,
— co-ordinating Community and international action,
— evaluating the impact of Community measures, and
— making parents, teachers and consumers aware of the dangers of Internet content and how they can minimise them.

The Action Plan has produced a number of ongoing projects in three areas : hotlines, filtering/rating, and awareness. The hotline projects are dealing with:

— education about, and prevention of, child pornography on the Internet,
— fighting child exploitation on the Internet,
— co-ordinating hotline providers in Europe,
— Denmark, Spain and Belgium as case-studies.[44]

In the field of filtering and rating, many of the projects build upon the ICRA labelling scheme referred to above and include smart card filtering, multilingual detection of racist and revisionist content, certification and rating of health information, a children's access Portal, and the development of a pan-European school-based Internet environment.[45] Finally, the Action Plan's awareness projects focus on younger and older children, and on the roles of parents and teachers.[46]

Notwithstanding the above-mentioned projects, the Action Plan has been criticised as vague and inconsequential, in particular in not defining the type of content with which the relevant initiatives were supposed to deal,[47] this despite the fact that the Commission itself has pointed out that,

[43] Article 152 (ex–129a) EC.

[44] http://www.europa.eu.int/information_society/programmes/iap/projects/hotlines/index_en.htm.

[45] http://www.europa.eu.int/information_society/programmes/iap/projects/filtering/euncle/index_en.htm.

[46] See also Commission, Creating a Safer Information Society by Improving the Security of Information Infrastructure and Combating Computer-related Crime, COM(2000) 890 (www.europa.eu.int/ispo), suggesting a series of non-legislative measures to encourage awareness and training amongst law enforcement agencies, Internet Service Providers, and consumer representatives.

[47] A Charlesworth, 'The Governance of the Internet in Europe', in Y Akdeniz, C Walker, and D Wall (eds), *The Internet, Law and Society* (Harlow, Longman, 2000) at 61.

'. . . it is crucial to differentiate between content which is illegal and other harmful content . . . The different categories of content pose radically different issues of principle, and call for very different legal and technological responses. . .'[48]

Perhaps in response to these criticisms, the Council extended the Action Plan,[49] and the Commission in 2004 proposed a Decision establishing a multiannual programme on promoting safer use of the Internet.[50] The Proposed Decision suggests four lines of action: first, fighting illegal content by building upon the hotline initiatives discussed above, in particular facilitating networking within Europe; second, tackling unwanted content, which involves funding content-rating and filtering technologies; third, promoting a safer environment, involving the development of Codes of Conduct; fourth, awareness-raising, particularly in regard to personalised, interactive and mobile applications.

Further Community action in support of self-help came with the adoption of the Directive on e-commerce of 2000,[51] which mandates Member States and the Commission to encourage:

'(a) the drawing-up of codes of conduct at Community level, by trade, professional and consumer associations or organisations, designed to contribute to the proper implementation of Articles 5 to 15.[52]

. . .

(e) the drawing up of codes of conduct regarding the protection of minors and human dignity.' (Article 16).

The final self-help initiative of note is the Council's 2000 Decision to combat child pornography on the Internet, mandating Member States to encourage Internet users to inform law enforcement authorities of online child pornography, and to ensure that law enforcement authorities can deal with complaints on a 24-hour basis and act swiftly on receipt of complaints.[53]

[48] Commission Internet Working Party, *Interim Report on Initiatives in EU Member States with Respect to Combating Illegal and Harmful Content on the Internet* (http://europa.eu.int/ISPO/legal/en/internet/internet.html, 1997).

[49] See now Decision No 1151/2003/EC of the European Parliament and of the Council amending Decision No 276/1999/EC adopting a multiannual Community action plan on promoting safer use of the Internet by combating illegal and harmful content on global networks. See also the report on the period 1999–2003 at COM(2003) 653.

[50] COM(2004) 91. The proposed legal basis is Article 153(2) EC.

[51] Chapter 2 note 35 above. Of course the Directive is aimed principally at ensuring a level playing-field for e-commerce: 'both existing and emerging disparities in Member States' legislation and case-law concerning liability of service providers acting as intermediaries prevent the smooth functioning of the Internal Market, in particularly impairing the development of cross-border services and producing distortions of competition', (Recital 40).

[52] Articles 5 to 15 include in particular the obligations relating to provision of information by service providers (Article 5) and by those making commercial communications (Article 6), including contact details, which can be important in ensuring that offensive material can be quickly disabled.

[53] OJ 2000 L138/1.

Substantive Protection

> 'Whatever the weight given to freedom of expression, the protection of minors and human dignity has always been a fundamental concern of media regulation.' *European Commission, Green Paper on the Protection of Minors and Human Dignity in Audiovisual and Information Services.*[54]

The Community has not adopted any measures offering substantive protection for consumers' morality interests in the context of e-commerce. Thus the question arises—what might the Community have done, or do? Certainly, any action restricting free speech would be fraught with the legal difficulties normally associated therewith, as well as the possibility of evasion through technical means.[55] The routing of all communications through a single state server, with centralised blacklisting, as adopted by some countries, seems entirely incompatible with the Community's commitment to free speech, as the European Commission has noted,

> 'Some third countries have introduced wide-ranging legislation to block all direct access to the Internet via access providers by introducing a requirement for 'proxy servers' similar to those used by large organisations for security reasons, combined with centralised blacklisting of documents, for reasons which go beyond the limited category of illegal content . . . Such a restrictive regime is inconceivable for Europe as it would severely interfere with the freedom of the individual and its political traditions.'[56]

There would seem to be two principal possibilities in respect of public control of online content: first, mandating providers to rate their own content; second, establishing a system of on-demand public rating.

A system of mandatory self-rating could be built upon the PICS architecture described above (Justices Rehnquist and O'Connor proposed a similar 'zoning' concept in *ACLU v Reno*).[57] Those providers failing to rate their content would see it blocked automatically by ISPs, and the State would have a residual role in checking the accuracy of ratings. It would provide some level of

[54] COM(96) 483 at 5.

[55] The general problem of evasion of control has of course caused States problems off-line—see for example the United Kingdom government's attempts to halt domestic sales of the book *Spycatcher*, which were frustrated in purpose because the book was freely available in the United States and other countries.

[56] *Communication to the European Parliament and Council on Illegal and Harmful Content on the Internet*, www2.echo.lu/legal/en/internet/content/communic.html. See also the subsequent Working Party Report at [*ibid.*] . . . /wpen.html, also Human Rights Watch, 'Freedom of Expression on the Internet', www.hrw.org/hrw/worldreport99/special/internet.html.

[57] Note 4 above, See also L Lessig, *Code: and Other Laws of Cyberspace* (New York, Basic Books, 1999). The core suggestion of both being that all pornography be zoned into a '.' domain.

autonomy for content-providers in self-rating, and enable users better to shield themselves from unwanted content.

However, the right to freedom of speech would seem to overwhelm any case for generalised mandatory self-rating within the Community. The European Court of Human Rights, long an arbiter of note to the Community,[58] has always been strict in its interpretation of Article 10(2) of the European Convention on Human Rights, which permits only those restrictions 'necessary in a democratic society'.[59] In *Ollson v Sweden*, the Court said that 'the notion of necessity implies that the interference corresponds to a pressing social need and, in particular, that it is proportionate . . .' Generalised mandatory self-rating would seem a *disproportionate* response to the problem of harmful Internet content, given that it would require a huge amount of innocuous speech to be rated.

The potential impact of mandated self-rating can also be illustrated by two cases from the United States. In the first, *McIntyre v Ohio Elections Commission*, the Supreme Court held unconstitutional a requirement that those distributing election materials state their names and addresses in those materials, ruling that it could only be lawful to compel speech if it served an overriding State interest, which was not the instant case.[60] In *Pacific Gas & Elec. Co. v Public Utils. Comm'n of California*,[61] the claimants challenged a requirement that they include certain information sheets about competitors with the bills they sent to customers; the US Supreme Court held this requirement unlawful as it required speakers to 'associate with speech with which [they] may disagree'[62] and to 'alter their speech to conform with an agenda they do not set'.[63]

A more feasible option than mandatory self-rating is on-demand public rating. Such a system has been adopted by Australia, under the Broadcasting Services Amendment (On Line Services) Act 1999 ('BSA Act 1999'),[64] which

[58] See in particular Case 36/75, *Rutili v Minister for the Interior* [1975] ECR 1219.

[59] See eg *Handyside v United Kingdom* ECtHRR A 24 (1976), 1 EHRR 737.

[60] 487 US 781 (1988); 108 S. CT. 2667 (at 1519–20). See also *Riley v National Federation of the Blind*, 514 US 334; 115 S.Ct. 1511 (1995), in which charity fundraisers successfully challenged a state requirement that they disclose to potential donors the percentage of donations given to charity. The Supreme Court held that mandating speech that a speaker would not otherwise make of itself restricts the right to free speech. See generally Weinberg 1997 note 33 above at 8.

[61] 475 US 1, 15 (1986); 106 S. Ct. 903.

[62] At 15; 911.

[63] At 9; 908. Although requirements of product labelling are alive and well, these can be distinguished from mandatory self-rating of content in as much as labelling always concerns objective information in a commercial context.

[64] Inserting a new Schedule 5 into the Broadcasting Services Act 1992, text available at http://www.aba.gov.au. See generally: L Edwards, 'The Problem of Intermediary Liability' in L Edwards (ed) *The New Legal Framework for E-Commerce in Europe* (Oxford, Hart, 2005); also ABA, 'Australia's Co-regulatory Scheme for Internet Content' (www.aba.gov.au/what/online/international.htm, August 2000).

brought Internet content generally within the classification framework there used for films. The Act requires that a restricted access system is put in place for material which is classified as unsuitable for minors by the Office for Film and Literature Classification.[65] Anyone can request that the Office classify particular material. ISPs must take all reasonable steps 'technically and commercially feasible' to block access by end-users to sites which contain material unsuitable for children which is not protected by access controls.[66] Whilst some ISPs use filters to block access themselves, it has been accepted that the supply of a filter to the consumer complies with the 'all reasonable steps' requirement above.[67] It should be noted that such blocking is not entirely effective *if* a site wants to evade it; speech can easily be 'mirrored', as happened in the *Radikal* case, which involved the German Public Prosecutor General requesting that all domestic Internet Service Providers block access to a Dutch site hosting *Radikal* magazine. The basis of the request was that the site allegedly promoted terrorist activities contrary to the German criminal code; the ISPs, under threat of prosecution, complied with the Prosecutor General's request; the site was subsequently copied to fifty or so 'mirror' sites around the world, largely negating the practical impact of the Prosecutor General's action.[68] However, the problems of mirroring in the commercial field are unlikely to be as extensive as in the non-commercial, given that the revenue streams of the former are more susceptible to attack.

The BSA Act 1999 also prohibits the domestic hosting of obscene material, namely that containing:

— detailed instruction in crime, violence or drug use;
— child pornography; bestiality;
— excessively violent or sexually violent material;
— real depictions of actual sexual activity.

Some of the domestic material acted against has moved abroad—the Australian Broadcasting Authority has not detailed how much, but certainly some has, for example the site *teenagers.com.au* moved its material to servers

[65] ABS Act 1992, Schedule 5, Sections 30–9, 82–3.

[66] ABS Act 1992, Schedule 5, Sections 40–51, 82–3.

[67] See generally, Commonwealth Scientific and Industrial Research Organisation, *Blocking Content on the Internet: A Technical Perspective*, http://www.cmis.csiro.au/projects+sectors/blocking.pdf.

[68] G Smith, *Internet Law and Regulation* (London, Sweet & Maxwell, 1997) at 252. The court of first instance was the Langericht Munchen I (Regional Court of Munich). Information from TKRNEWS-L e-mail newsletter of 17 November 1999, archived at www.listserv.gmd.de/archives/tkrnews-l.html. It is possible that the publicity surrounding the matter actually harmed the German interest in suppressing the material and therein lies an interesting parallel with state censorship of pop songs in the UK—it is often said that one of the most effective marketing techniques is to have them banned by the (state-run) BBC.

in the United States.[69] (Filtering nevertheless serves to protect *Australian* consumers in respect of such material.)

The BSA Act 1999 appears to be functioning well. An Australian Broadcasting Authority (ABA) report of August 2000 detailed the scheme's first six months of operation:

— the ABA received approximately 200 complaints,
— most of these were about the Web, the remainder about Usenet newsgroups,
— about 70 complaints concerned domestic content,
— of those 70 complaints, 60 resulted in take-down notices,
— of the 130 foreign items complained about, 100 have been notified to the makers of approved filters,
— over half of the instances of prohibited content concerned the offensive depiction of a minor.[70]

It is arguable that the Community should, on the basis of its internal market competence, copy Australia by mandating its Member States to institute a system of on-demand public rating. Such novel action by the Community would no doubt be controversial as regards legal competence,[71] yet the evidence above suggests that consumer confidence, and thus the internal market, is adversely affected by the open availability of online material unsuitable for children.

Such a measure would restrict free speech, but could be considered proportionate given that providers can easily inform adult consumers about the nature of the goods and services they offer, without those consumers first having to prove their adult status, and that proving adult status is generally not onerous. Various effective controls are available, including credit cards and customised free age-verification services such as *cyberage.com.*

Requiring proof-of-age cannot be considered to undermine the principal rationales of the right to free speech, described by Eric Barendt as being: (a) a necessary foundation to the search for truth, (b) an essential ingredient of effective participative democracy, and (c) an aspect of individual self-fulfilment.[72] Whilst generally powerful, these rationales are not persuasive objections to the interest of parents in having commercially-produced violent or sexual material screened from their children; it would be somewhat fanciful to argue that such screening either significantly (a) hinders the search for truth

[69] See further in relation to the move of the teenager.com.au site, http://www.wired.com/news/politics/0,1283,34043,00.html, both sites visited 26/08/00.

[70] Note 64 above, at 9.

[71] The Open Method of Coordination might be regarded as a more natural route of control. See generally on the OMC: C de la Porte, 'Is the Open Method of Co-ordination Appropriate for Organising Activities at European Level in Sensitive Policy Areas?,' (2002) 8 *European Law Journal* 38.

[72] *Freedom of Speech* (Oxford, Clarendon Press, 1985) at 20.

(the search goes on by adults), or (b) undermines participative democracy (children are not significant political actors), or (c) impairs individual autonomy (self-expression remains possible, just not to children in respect of such online material). Similar arguments underlie the controls on the distribution of adult material off-line. Indeed, the rationales of the right to free speech can be argued to have less force generally in the specific context of commerce, given that the latter is predominantly concerned with selling rather than searching for truth, expressing political ideas, or expressing the self.

The institution of on-demand public rating would not result in the disappearance of consumers' fears about online content. However, it would enable the machinery of the Community (in particular the Commission where Member States fail to comply with their obligations) to be brought to bear more easily against some harmful material, and such action would have value in reassuring consumers that their concerns are taken seriously at Community level.

The Preservation Provisions of the Directive on E-Commerce

Although the Community has failed to offer concrete protection to consumers' moral interests within the electronic environment, chapter 2 above noted the E-commerce Directive's[73] general scheme of home country control of 'Information Society services',[74] and in that light the Directive's preservation provisions are here worthy of note. The Directive expressly preserves the right of Member States to restrict such services emanating from another Member State for reasons of:

> — public policy, in particular the prevention, investigation, detection and prosecution of criminal offences, including the protection of minors and the fight against any incitement to hatred on grounds of race, sex, religion or nationality, and violations of human dignity concerning individual persons,
> — the protection of public health,
> — public security including the safeguarding of national security and defence,
> — the protection of consumers, including investors. (Article 3(4)).[75]

[73] Chapter 2 note 53 above.

[74] The Directive defines 'information society services', as, 'any service normally provided for remuneration, at a distance, by electronic means and at the individual request of a recipient of services' (Article 2(a)). The Preamble to the Directive makes it clear that the services do not have to be remunerated by individual users (but may, for example, be remunerated by advertising): 'information society services . . . extend to services which are not remunerated by those who receive them', (Recital 18).

[75] Also of note is Article 1(6) of the E-commerce Directive, providing, 'this Directive does not affect measures taken at Community or national level, in the respect of Community law, in order to promote cultural and linguistic diversity and to ensure the defence of pluralism.' Thus laws such as the French *Loi Tubon* (Law No. 94–665), mandating a certain degree of use of a national language in the media, would seem to be unaffected by the Directive (the *Loi Tubon* was adopted pursuant to Article 2 of the Constitution, which identifies French as the official language of the Republic, but was struck down by the Conseil d'Etat in as far as it applied to private-sector speech).

Measures taken in derogation of the general prohibition on restricting services from another Member State must be preceded, except in an emergency, by a request to the 'home' Member State to act against the offending service provider, and by notification to the Commission, which is explicitly charged with the duty of examining such measures for compatibility with Community law; if the Commission finds that the measures breach Community law, then it has the power to act against the Member State in question in accordance with the procedure laid down in Article 155 of the EC Treaty.[76] From the point of view of consumer confidence, the explicit mention in Article 3(4) above of the right of Member States to restrict information society services for reasons of child protection is particularly positive.

Observations

The Community has given significant support to consumer self-help in the field of morality interests, in particular encouraging the use of filters in a variety of languages, funding the development of filtering standards which are acceptable across Europe, and mandating the Commission and the Member States to draw up codes of conduct to protect minors. However, this support can be criticised as vague, and as no substitute for substantive action. In the latter area, the Community has failed to take any action. Although there is a question mark over its competence in the field, it is arguable that the Community should copy Australia in instituting a system of on-demand public rating by Member States of online content unsuitable for children. Whilst this would not have provided any kind of panacea to the problem of harmful content, it would have had some impact, in particular indicating to consumers that their interests are taken seriously at the European level.

Although it might be argued that content control is a culturally-sensitive area in which the Community can only be expected to move slowly, intellectual property is also a culturally-sensitive area, and, as the chapters below will show, the Community has there moved quickly to protect *producers'* interests.

[76] Article 3(4)(b).

5

Producers I—Authorship Interests

Threats to Producers' Authorship Interests

The online threats to authors' ability to control *reproductions* of their original work are driven by two technical features of the Internet in particular. The first is the speed with which such work can be found and copied, aided by search tools, hyper-links, file compression technology and large bandwidths. The second is the ability of users to act anonymously, both in posting and copying. Of course, producers' problems in an online context are no different in form to those off-line (which have never come close to collapsing the legitimate market for original work), but there is a difference of scale. Off-line copying is typically done through a primitive type of exchange of *authorised* copies, eg a group of friends making unauthorised copies of each other's CDs. In practice, this places limits on the numbers of copies which are made. The Net removes those limits. One copy on a server can spawn an almost limitless number of unauthorised copies.

Authors often have little power to control copying carried out in the course of online access to authorised copies; this includes copying from cache memory (the memory of individual computers, vital to the Internet's speed of operation, used to store Web-pages accessed in the previous hour or so).[1] Whilst in the off-line world art galleries can forbid photography and concert-goers can be checked for recording devices, such controls are not generally possible online.[2]

A good example of the problems that authors face can be found in the field of music, seemingly the type of online work with most economic significance at present and a highly sought-after commodity by online consumers—music artists and KaZaa (file-sharing software) counted for six of the *Yahoo!* Top Ten Searches in August 2003 and four of those in September 2004.[3] File-swapping is facilitated by MP3 technology, which can be used to compress three minutes of music into approximately 3 MB of memory. These files can be transmitted quickly across the Net, to be played on consumers' computers, or on dedicated MP3 players (the legality of which has been unsuccessfully challenged in the United States).[4] The file-swapping service *Napster*[5] had 8 million users before being closed down as a peer-to-peer—'P2P'—service in 2001.[6] As a P2P service-provider *Napster* acted as a distributor of software which enabled users interested in particular music to find it in the computer memory of other online users. Despite the high-profile closure of *Napster*, other file-swapping services such as *Bearshare.com* have since continued to operate freely.

The problem of unauthorised copying is also visible in the field of software. One study of the download logs of a server holding an unauthorised copy of a software program found that there had been 600,000 downloads over the course of six months,[7] and it was estimated in 1999 that 60 per cent of the software sales on *eBay*'s auction site in the United States were of unauthorised copies.[8] This pattern reflects experience offline; in some Asian countries pirate sales of copyright material have been estimated as constituting 90 per cent of

[1] See generally PB Hugenholtz and K Koelman, 'Online Service Provider Liability for Copyright Infringement,' Paper delivered at WIPO Workshop on Service Provider Liability (www.wipo.int/eng/meetings/1999/osp/, December 1999).

[2] 'Trusted systems' and other access-control mechanisms are discussed below.

[3] http://buzz.yahoo.com/.

[4] *Recording Industry Association of America Inc v Diamond Multimedia Systems Inc* 180F.3rd 10772 (9th Circuit Court of Appeals, 15/June/1999), http://laws.findlaw.com/9th/9856727.html. The case had some similarity with the copyright-based challenge to video recorders issued by television companies in *Sony Corp. of America v Universal City Studios* 464 US 417 (1984). See generally on copyright and the Internet: JP Barlow, 'The Economy of Ideas', www.eff.org/~barlow/economyofideas.html.

[5] www.napster.com.

[6] *A & M Records Inc v Napster Inc.* (USDC No Cal., 5 May 2000). Napster was subsequently acquired by Roxio Inc., which now runs it as a private online music enterprise (not 'peer-to-peer').

[7] Oktay B and Wrenn G, *A look back at the notice-takedown provisions of the US Digital Millennium Copyright Act one year after enactment* (WIPO, www.wipo.int/eng/meetings/1999/osp/, 1999) at 13. (It should be noted that the study was conducted by a software manufacturer, Adobe Systems, and the software in question was its product Adobe Acrobat.)

[8] Cnet news, *Software pirates doing brisk trade on auction*, http://news.cnet.com/news//0–1007–200–346607.html, 30/8/99.

all sales.[9] It can be expected that as technology develops, the problems affecting music and software will also begin seriously to affect film.

Another form of copying which defeats the authorship interest is that of 'inlining', where a third party Web-site 'frames' the original work of another site and defeats that site's ability to capture the revenue from it. A good example of inlining is provided by the facts of *Shetland Times v Wills,*[10] in which the defendant published an online newspaper, with direct hypertext links to stories on the claimant's Web site. The links allowed the reader to by-pass the front page of the claimant's Web site, which was the revenue-producing part of the site. (The case was eventually settled, although the claimant was successful in obtaining an interim injunction against the defendant.)

Material authorship interests are also challenged by the Net's capacity to support illicit *access* to original work. Chargeable provision of original work is an important part of the electronic marketplace—pay-TV was in 1998 the largest revenue-producing part of film-making in Europe.[11] Whilst in the off-line world the physical identification and processing of people is a simple and easy-to-use access filter, online identification is more difficult, as is discussed further in the section on 'self-help' below.

Finally, *re-use* of original work, which does not involve reproduction or unauthorised access per se, is facilitated by the Internet. When original work is placed online, it can be substantially and materially exploited by third parties (as it can off-line of course). A good example of such 'free-riding' is given by the facts of *British Horseracing Board Ltd and Others v William Hill Organsiation Ltd.*:[12] the claimants employed 80 people to provide information regarding horse-racing on their Web-sites. The information provided was re-used by the defendant bookmakers in their online gambling business without any compensation being paid to the claimants [the case is discussed further in the section below entitled 'Controlling Reuse—the Database Directive'].

Self-help as a Solution?

Ejan Mackaay has drawn a parallel between the historical establishment of property rights in land and the potential of technology to enable authors to

[9] Commentary, (April 2000) *Electronic Business Law* at 13.

[10] 1997 SC 316. Trademark law has also been used in this regard, see *Ticketmaster v Microsoft* CV 97–3055 RAP (CDE Cal, 28 April 1997), which eventually settled, with Microsoft agreeing not to 'deep-link' into Ticketmaster's site.

[11] Commission, *Globalisation and the Information Society—The Need for Strengthened International Co-ordination* (COM(98) 50) at 16.

[12] *The Times*, 23 February 2001, (High Court); www.courtservice.gov.uk.

'build their own fences',[13] fences which would consist essentially of conditional access systems based on technological protection devices and on passwords. These systems are largely effective in protecting authors' access interest in relation to information services, as can be seen by their long-term successful use by many sites.[14] Yet conditional access systems are not a panacea to the threats to authors' interests outlined above. Once access has been granted to a legitimate user, the author in question cannot then unilaterally control what the user does with the material, which may be reproduced or reused without consent. Further, access controls can be circumvented by illicit technology and by illicitly obtained passwords.[15]

Digital technology does enable producers to identify individual copies of original work. Data can be minutely and uniquely altered in ways that are difficult or impossible for third parties to discover—techniques variously known as tattooing, fingerprinting or watermarking.[16] These techniques enable producers to identify whether a particular copy is held by a legitimate purchaser, and thus to identify unauthorised copies. However, the ability to identify unauthorised copies does not of itself enable authors to protect their interests—this is only the case where that ability exists in conjunction with legal regulation.

Charles Clark, General Counsel to the International Publishers' Copyright Council, has said that 'the answer to the machine is in the machine'.[17] He has not been alone in predicting that trusted systems may develop, enabling authors to ensure that their work is only transmitted to consumers whose systems cannot copy it without authorisation, ie the author's system would check that the consumer's system was compliant with the author's demands before transmission. Larry Lessig has written that, 'Code can, and increasingly will, displace law as the primary defence of intellectual property in cyberspace. Private fences not public law . . .'[18] However, such trusted systems do not yet

[13] E Mackaay, 'The Economics of Emergent Property Rights on the Internet,' in PB Hugenholtz (ed), *The Future of Copyright in a Digital Environment* (The Hague, Kluwer Law International, 1999) at 20.

[14] There are many examples of such, eg ft.com.

[15] See generally, International Bureau of WIPO, *Existing international, regional and national legislation concerning the protection of the rights of broadcasting organizations* (www.wipo.int/eng/meetings/1998/sccr_98/index.htm, September 1998) at 26. For some time the site *passwords.com* operated as a resource for those seeking to gain free access to password-controlled sites (it now operates as a pornography site).

[16] See Commission, *Green Paper on copyright in the information society*, COM(95) 382 at paras 49–50. See also Commission, *Follow-up to the Green Paper on Copyright and Related Rights in the Information Society*, COM(96) 586 at chapters 2–3; T Vinje, 'A Brave New World of Technical Protection Systems: Will There Still be Room for Copyright?' [1996] 18 *European Intellectual Property Review* 431.

[17] C Clark, 'The Answer to the Machine is in the Machine', in Hugenholtz, note 13 above, at 139.

[18] *Code and Other Laws of Cyberspace* (New York, Basic Books, 1999) at 126.

exist. Despite a myriad of technological possibilities, there would seem to be a historical trend towards individuals having ever-wider access to advanced technology, and this trend does not bode well for the prospects of effective technological protection of original work. Although it is somewhat dangerous to try to predict how technology will develop, it can be noted that the software, music and film industries have for many years sought to develop copy-proof technology and generally failed. The most recent technological initiative of the film industry to prevent unauthorised copying—the DVD—suffered a setback when its algorithm was broken in 1999 and put on various Web-sites for the public to copy.[19] Although the person who posted the algorithm was successfully sued for so doing,[20] the information spread quickly and widely.

The idea of the 'trusted system' is superficially attractive, but it is difficult to see how even that could ever guard entirely against unauthorised copying. If a work is to be enjoyed by consumers, it is in theory susceptible to copying, ie if a consumer can hear or see the material, then so can a machine. Technology alone can provide only part of the solution to the threats to authors' interests outlined above.

Community Regulation

> 'The existence of a Single Market for new products and services is vital for the development of the Information Society in Europe. It will contribute towards generating new products and services that have a diversity of content, which is essential to attract users on a large scale. The Single Market must offer adequate and secure investment conditions and legal security.' *European Commission, Follow-up to the Green Paper on Copyright and Related Rights in the Information Society.*[21]

The Community has succeeded in providing a broad framework for the protection of authors' interests, adopting three instruments of particular relevance—the Information Society Directive,[22] the Directive on conditional access services,[23] and the Database Directive.[24] These instruments will now be discussed in turn.

[19] See www.qlinks.net/items/qlitem5681.htm.

[20] *Universal City Studios Inc et v Reimerdes,* US District Court S.D New York, 20 January 2000, (April 2000) *Electronic Business Law* at 13.

[21] Note 16 above, at 2.

[22] Directive 2001/29/EC on the harmonisation of copyright and certain related rights in the information society, OJ 2001 L167/10.

[23] Directive 98/84/EC.

[24] Directive 96/9/EC on the legal protection of databases.

Controlling Reproduction—the Information Society Directive[25]

The Information Society Directive was adopted in February 2001, and followed a number of earlier measures dealing with highly specific aspects of copyright and related rights, including:

— Directive 91/250/EEC on the Legal Protection of Computer Programmes,[26]
— Directive 92/100/EEC on Rental Right and on Lending Right and on Certain Rights related to Copyright in the Field of Intellectual Property,[27]
— Directive 93/83/EEC on the co-ordination of certain rules concerning Copyright and Rights Related to Copyright Applicable to Satellite Broadcasting and Cable Retransmission,[28]
— Directive 93/98/EEC Harmonising the Term of Copyright and Certain Related Rights, defining relevant periods of protection.[29]

The Information Society Directive is closely modelled on, and designed partially to implement, the World Copyright Treaty 1996 ('WCT') and the World Performances and Phonograms Treaty 1996 ('WPPT').[30]

The Directive offers support for self-help in a number of ways. First, it imposes on Member States an obligation to take steps to provide adequate legal protection against the circumvention of 'effective technological measures' designed to protect copyright and related rights,

> 'Member States shall provide adequate legal protection against the circumvention of any effective technological measures, which the person concerned carries out in the knowledge, or with reasonable grounds to know, that he or she pursues that objective.' Article 6(1).[31]

[25] Note 22 above. See also Commission, *Proposal for a Directive on the harmonisation of certain aspects of copyright and related rights in the Information Society*, COM (1999) 250, May 1999 (see also the original, 1997 Proposal, COM(97) 628, http://europa.eu.int/comm/dg15/en/intprop/intprop/index.htm, and Parliament's Report of 10 February 1999 A4–0026/99 ('the Barzanti Report')).

[26] OJ 1991 L122/42.

[27] OJ 1992 L346/61.

[28] OJ 1993 L248/15.

[29] OJ 1993 L290/9.

[30] Recital 15 and Proposal, note 25 above, at 3. See generally on the WCT and WPPT, S Lai, 'Recent Developments in Copyright, Database Protection and (Online) Licensing' (1999) 7(1) *International Journal of Law & Information Technology* 73.

[31] Limited exceptions are provided to this general prohibition in Article 6(1), including in regard to libraries (Article 5(2)(b)), private teaching or research purposes (Article 5(3)(a)), and to use by disabled people (Article 5(3)(c)). See also corresponding WCT Article 11: 'contracting parties shall provide adequate legal protection and effective legal remedies against the circumvention of effective legal remedies against the circumvention of effective technological measures that are used by authors in connection with the exercise of their rights under this Treaty . . .'; and Article 18 WPPT. <http://europa.eu.int/comm/dg15/en/intprop/indprop/922.htm>.

Effective technological measures are defined as:

> 'any technology, device or component that, in the normal course of its operation, is designed to prevent or restrict acts, in respect of works or other subject-matter, which are not authorised by the rightholder of any copyright or right related to copyright . . .' (Article 6(3)).

Activity ancillary to the use of devices or services designed to circumvent technological protection systems is prohibited in wide terms:

> '[Member States must provide] . . . protection against the manufacture, import, distribution, sale, rental, advertisement for sale or rental, or possession for commercial purposes of devices, products or components or the provision of services which:
> (a) are promoted, advertised or marketed for the purpose of circumvention of, or
> (b) have only a limited commercially significant purpose or use other than to circumvent, or
> (c) are primarily designed, produced, adapted or performed for the purpose of enabling or facilitating the circumvention of, any effective technological measures.' (Article 6(2)).

The second limb of support for self-help is in Article 7 of the Directive, which prohibits the removal or alteration of electronic rights-management information as well as knowingly dealing with material which has had such information removed or altered.[32] The scope of Article 7 is necessarily linked to a breach of copyright, so that it is lawful for example to remove rights-management information from material retained purely for personal use—the provision applies where the person removing the rights-management information, 'knows, or has reasonable grounds to know, that by so doing he is inducing, enabling, facilitating or concealing an infringement of any copyright . . .' (Article 7(1)). Thus the ability of authors to identify copies, whether for purely informational purposes or for the assertion of legal rights, is protected.

In terms of protecting authors' substantive interests, the Directive provides a trio of rights. First, in respect of reproduction:

> 'Member States shall provide for the exclusive right to authorise or prohibit direct or indirect, temporary or permanent reproduction by any means and in any form, in whole or in part: (a) for authors, of their works . . .'[33]

The reproduction right is subject to only one mandatory exception, that for 'transient reproductions having no independent economic significance and forming an essential part of a communications chain' (Article 5(1))—this allows the making of cache copies, which was judged to be essential to

[32] See also corresponding Articles 19 WPPT and 12 WCT.
[33] Article 2.

maintaining the Internet's speed of operation.[34] The ability to store cache copies means that where users jump back to documents they have recently accessed, their servers do not have to re-request the documents, thus freeing-up valuable network capacity. Cache copies can be extracted by those with the necessary technological know-how. The limitation of the exception to 'essential' reproductions with 'no independent economic significance' emphasises the Community's focus on authors' material interests and may even create an impetus towards technical change making cache copies a non-essential part of the Internet.[35]

The second right designed to protect authors' substantive interest is that of communication to the public:

> 'Member States shall provide authors with the exclusive rights to authorise or prohibit any communication to the public of their works, by wire or wireless means, including the making available to the public of their works in such a way that members of the public may access them from a place and at a time individually chosen by them.'[36]

The third right is that of distribution:

> 'Member States shall provide for authors, in respect of the original of their works or of copies thereof, the exclusive right to authorise or prohibit any form of distribution to the public by sale or otherwise.'[37]

The reproduction and communication to the public rights are subject to a definitive list of optional limitations, in summary:

(a) use for teaching or scientific research,
(b) uses for those who have a disability,
(c) reproduction by the press,
(d) quotations for purposes such as criticism or review,
(e) use for the purposes of public security,
(f) use of political speeches as well as extracts of public lectures or similar works,
(g) use during religious ceremonies,
(h) use of works, such as works of architecture, made to be located permanently in public places,

[34] Proposal, note 25 above, at para 4(1).

[35] Compare the Directive on e-commerce (chapter 2 note 35 above), which exempts information service providers from liability for the 'automatic, intermediate and temporary storage of . . . information, performed for the sole purpose of making more efficient the information's onward transmission to other recipients at their request', (Article 13(1)), this exemption is lost if the service provider becomes aware that the original source of the material has been removed from the network or access to it has been barred and the provider does not itself act expeditiously to remove it or bar access. This regime is broadly similar to that in the US under the Digital Millennium Copyright Act 1999 (17 USC Title II).

[36] Article 3.

[37] Article 4.

(i) incidental inclusion of a work in other material,
(j) use for the purpose of advertising the public exhibition or sale of artistic works,
(k) use for the purpose of caricature, parody or pastiche,
(l) use in connection with the demonstration or repair of equipment,
(m) use of an artistic work in the form of a building or drawing for the purposes of reconstructing the building,
(n) use by communication or making available, for private study, by libraries and comparable institutions,
(o) use in certain other cases of minor importance where exceptions already exist in national law, provided that they only concern analogue use. (Article 5(3)).[38]

Whilst the list of exceptions is long, and authors would have benefited from a greater degree of harmonisation,[39] it is an optional list, which is surprising given that the exceptions are generally well-established (the Berne Convention 1886 made provision for all of them) and that they only apply:

> 'to certain specific cases and shall not be interpreted in such a way as to allow their application to be used in a manner which unreasonably prejudices the rightholders' legitimate interests or conflicts with the normal exploitation of their works or other subject matter.'[40]

The limitations in Article 5(2)(a) and (b) relating to reprography and private use are made subject to authors obtaining 'fair compensation'—a reference to levies on blank recording media and the like.[41] However, this right to compensation is not absolute, Recital 35 provides that a 'valuable criterion' in evaluating the level of compensation would be 'the possible harm resulting from the act in question,' and that where 'rightholders have already received payment in some other form, for instance as part of a licence fee, no specific payment or separate payment may be due.'

As noted above, the list of exceptions is finite in respect of digital material (Article 5(3)(p) provides a further exception for 'use in other cases of minor importance where exceptions already exist under national law, provided these

[38] Although neither this book nor the Directive focus on authors' moral interests, it can be noted that the optional limitations do make some provision for these: exceptions (a), (c), (d), (f) and (k) above provide that the author's name shall be indicated 'unless this proves impossible.' (Contrast the wording of the Proposal, note 25 above—'whenever possible'.)

[39] See generally H MacQueen, 'Copyright and the Internet', in L Edwards and C Waelde (eds), *Law and the Internet* (Oxford, Hart Publishing, 2000), who details the differing views of the Member States as to the desirability of such a long list, at 215. Recital 22 states, 'it is desirable that Member States should arrive at a coherent application of these exceptions, which will be assessed when reviewing implementing legislation in the future.'

[40] Compare the corresponding provision of the Berne Convention 1886: reproduction may be allowed 'in certain special cases, provided that such exploitation does not conflict with a normal exploitation of the work and does not unreasonably prejudice the legitimate interests of the author', (Article 9(2)).

[41] The UK long-resisted this change in its law: W Cornish, *Intellectual Property* (London, Sweet & Maxwell, 1999) paras 13–17.

only affect analogue uses'). It is not immediately clear from Article 5 whether these exceptions are rights in themselves or merely defences to claims of infringement. This is important as if they are merely defences to claims of infringement then if producers have the technical means to prevent use, then they will be able to do so. Article 6(4) would seem to indicate that the exceptions are indeed merely defences, it regulates the possibility of exclusion of users from the benefit of a number of exceptions, the most important of which from the point of view of the average user is that of reproduction for private use;[42] Member States may *only* take appropriate measures to ensure that rightholders make the exception available to beneficiaries where—

— there is an absence of voluntary measures taken by rightholders,
— the beneficiary has legal access to the material,
— reproduction for private use has not already been made possible,
— not in relation to material made available to the public on agreed contractual terms in such a way that members of the public may access it from a place and at a time individually chosen by them. [43]

As MacQueen has noted,[44] various aspects of the prohibition of action in the presence of voluntary measures by rightholders are unclear:

— how long must a Member State wait before taking action?
— can a Member State take action against a rightholder based in another Member State?
— how difficult can a rightholder make it for a consumer to benefit from Article 6(4)?

In relation to the last question above, it might be imagined that rightholders would be likely to make it difficult indeed for consumers to benefit, for example, by requiring written forms to be filled in and sent through the post etc. The Directive could usefully have included some express provision on the matter. Most importantly, the rightholder can condition legal access to the work, an a priori requirement for the operation of the exception, on the conclusion of a contract with the beneficiary, which can be used to negate the operation of the exception itself.

[42] The others are reprography, library, archiving of broadcasts, reproduction of broadcasts by social institutions, teaching and research, the disabled, and public security and the performance or reporting of administrative, parliamentary or judicial proceedings (in relation to the reproduction right); where the first, second and third indents of Article 6(4) noted in the text above are satisfied, the Directive *compels* Member States to take appropriate measures to ensure that rightholders make available the benefit of the exception; and the same is true in relation to the communication and making available rights as regards the latter three exceptions above.

[43] This provision was not included in the Proposal, note 25 above, which sought to prohibit all circumvention without authority.

[44] Note 39 above, at 217.

The Directive's trio of rights—reproduction, communication and distribution—clearly offer at least formal protection for authors' interests from the threats discussed above. The posting of unauthorised copies of original work on Web-sites, whether for reward or not, will infringe the author's reproduction and communication to the public rights (but not the distribution right, which refers 'exclusively to fixed copies that can be put into circulation as tangible objects').[45] The facilitation of copying of original work by file-swapping services such as *Napster* would seem, at least once notice has been given by copyright holders,[46] to infringe the reproduction right.

The reproduction, communication and distribution rights are reinforced by a powerful remedial regime. Article 8(1) stipulates that, 'Member States shall provide sanctions which are effective, proportionate and dissuasive', a provision paralleled in Part III of the WTO/TRIPS Agreement on Enforcement of Intellectual Property Rights. The use of the term 'dissuasive', applying over and above the general Community law duty of Member States to ensure the effectiveness of remedies,[47] might be thought to imply that Member States are obliged to institute criminal penalties, but the point is moot.[48] Article 8(2) further provides that rightholders whose interests are prejudiced by infringing activity must be able to: 'bring an action for damages and/or apply for an injunction and, where appropriate, have the infringing material seized.' These enforcement provisions have since been buttressed by Directive 2004/48 on the enforcement of intellectual property rights, which is discussed below.

In contrast to the two years given to Member States to implement the Directive on distance contracts discussed in chapter 2 above, the Information Society Directive gives Member States eighteen months[49] (one of the final amendments introduced by the Parliament).[50]

Controlling Access—the Directive on Conditional Access Services

The Community has acted to protect authors' interest in controlling access to original work through the adoption of Directive 98/84 on conditional access

[45] Proposal, note 25 above, at 27.

[46] This is the approach taken by the US courts under parallel legislation, see the *Napster* case, note 6 above.

[47] Case 14/83, *Von Colson and Kamann v Land Nordrhein-Westfalen* [1984] ECR 1891. See generally, F Snyder, 'The effectiveness of European Community Law' (1993) 56 *Modern Law Review* 19.

[48] Compare Articles 61 TRIPS: 'Members shall provide for criminal procedures and penalties to be applied at least in cases of . . . copyright piracy on a commercial scale.'

[49] Article 13(1).

[50] See European Parliament legislative resolution on the Council common position for adopting a European Parliament and Council directive on the harmonisation of certain aspects of copyright and related rights in the Information Society (9512/1/2000–C5–0520/2000–1997/0359 (COD)).

services,[51] which reflects various aspects of the 1994 WTO/TRIPS Agreement. The scope of the Directive is identified as covering any of the following services when provided against remuneration and on a conditional access basis:

> '— television broadcasting, as defined in point (a) of Article 1 of Directive 89/552/EC;
> — radio broadcasting, meaning any transmission by wire or over the air, including that by satellite, of radio programmes intended for reception by the public;[52]
> — Information Society services within the meaning of Article 1(2) of Council Directive 98/34/EC of the European Parliament and of the Council of 22 June 1998[53] laying down a procedure for the provision of information in the field of technical standards and regulations and of rules on information society services . . .' (Article 2(a)).

It is clear from Article 2(a) above that the Directive covers services such as pay-TV and directly-remunerated information provision. Article 4 imposes a duty on Member States to prohibit the counterfeiting of access-control devices:

> 'Member States shall prohibit on their territory all of the following activities:
> (a) the manufacture, import, distribution, sale, rental or possession for commercial purposes of illicit devices;[54]
> (b) the installation, maintenance or replacement for commercial purposes of an illicit device;
> (c) the use of commercial communications to promote illicit devices.' (Article 4).[55]

As with the Information Society Directive's protection of technological protection devices, Article 4 provides authors with protection against the whole spectrum of commercialisation of illicit devices. It does not penalise the mere use of illicit devices as users may often not realise that their device is illicit. In any event the method of sanctioning traders should be sufficient to prevent the

[51] Note 23 above. See also Commission, *Green Paper on the Legal Protection of Encrypted Services in the Internal Market* (COM(96) 76); Commission, *Proposal for a European Parliament and Council Directive on the Legal Protection of Services based on, or consisting of, Conditional Access Services* ('Proposal') COM(97) 356; Council Common Position at OJ 1998 C262/34. The issue of encryption, as that of data protection, lay previously within the remit of the Council of Europe, see Council of Europe Recommendation R(91)14 on the legal protection of encrypted television services.

[52] The reference to 'radio broadcasting' in the second indent of Article 2(a) includes not only sound signals but 'possibly also data signals within the same channel,' *per* Proposal, note 51 above, at 12. The definitions of radio and television broadcasting do not include on-demand services, which come within the scope of the third indent, 'Information Society services'.

[53] OJ 1998 L204/37.

[54] The definition of 'illicit device' revolves around the use to which a device is put: '*illicit device* means any equipment or software designed or adapted to give access to a protected service in an intelligible form without the authorisation of the service provider', (Article 1(e)).

[55] The list of prohibited activities is taken from Principle I of the Council of Europe Recommendation R(91)14 on the legal protection of encrypted television services. The Recommendation also distinguishes between possession for private purposes and possession for commercial purposes, providing that only the latter is unlawful.

use of illicit devices, and thus to penalise use as well might be regarded as infringing the Community law principle of proportionality.[56]

This protection is reinforced, as in the case of the Information Society Directive,[57] through the duty placed on Member States to provide for effective remedies:

> 'Article 3 (1) Each Member State shall take the measures necessary to prohibit on its territory the activities listed in Article 4, and to provide for the sanctions and remedies listed in Article 5.
>
> Article 5 (1) The sanctions shall be effective, dissuasive and proportionate to the potential impact of the infringing activity.
>
> (2) Member States shall take the necessary measures to ensure that providers of protected services whose interests are affected by an infringing activity as specified in Article 4, carried out on their territory, have access to appropriate remedies, including bringing an action for damages and obtaining an injunction or other preventive measure, and where appropriate, applying for disposal outside commercial channels of illicit devices.'[58]

Article 5 thus prevents a Member State using the foreign *locus* of damage as a ground to refuse jurisdiction over an alleged infringement of the rights provided for by the Directive; the fact that the infringing activity is carried out on its territory is sufficient to establish jurisdiction.

It is clear from the Directive on conditional access services that the Community has provided early (1998) and comprehensive protection of producers' interests in controlling access.

Controlling Reuse—the Database Directive

The Community protects authors' reuse interest through the Database Directive 1996.[59] The Directive 'concerns the legal protection of databases in any form', and defines 'database' as 'a collection of independent works, data or other materials arranged in a systematic or methodical way and individually accessible by electronic or other means.'[60] Recital 17 elaborates on this definition:

[56] (Requiring that Community action goes no further than is necessary to achieve its aim). See generally, G de Búrca, 'The Principle of Proportionality and its Application in EC Law' (1993) 13 *Yearbook of European Law* 105.

[57] See the discussion of Article 8(1) of the Information Society Directive, page 104 above.

[58] Provision for seizure is also made by Article 7 of Directive 91/250/EEC on the Legal Protection of Computer Programmes, note 29 above. Article 5(2) above closely follows Articles 44 to 46 of the TRIPS Agreement.

[59] Note 24 above. Compare Article 10(2) of the TRIPS Agreement, and the Draft WIPO Database Treaty (www.wipo.org/eng/diploconf/6dc_all.htm). See generally, P Hugenholtz, 'The New Database Right: Early Case-Law from Europe' (http://www.ivir.nl/, April 2001).

[60] Article 1.

> 'whereas the term 'database' should be understood to include literary, artistic, musical or other collections of works or collections of other material such as texts, sound, images, numbers, facts, and data; whereas it should cover collections of independent works, data, or other materials which are systematically or methodically arranged and can be individually accessed; whereas this means that a recording or an audio-visual, cinematographic, literary or musical work as such does not fall within the scope of this Directive.'

The above definition is wide enough to include even a single Web page.[61] The Explanatory Memorandum to the original Proposal for a Directive described its aim as that of protecting work in relation to 'information in the widest sense of that term'.[62]

The individual elements comprising a database must be 'independent' and 'individually accessible by electronic or other means' (thus films and similar collections of interdependent data are excluded).[63] However, according to Recital 21, 'it is not necessary for those materials to have been physically stored in an organised manner'. Thus, any digital collection of data comes within the scope of the Directive, as long as the user is capable of retrieving individual pieces of data.

This requirement is clearly met by most, or all, commercial databases, in particular given that it can include 'either the obtaining, verification or presentation of the contents' of the database.

The Directive protects the re-use interest in databases through a sui generis 'database right', the first of its kind in the world. The right accrues where there has been 'qualitatively and/or quantitatively a substantial investment in either the obtaining, verification or presentation of the contents . . .'[64] The right is to:

> 'prevent extraction and/or re-utilization of the whole or of a substantial part, evaluated qualitatively and/or quantitatively, of the contents of the database.' (Article 7(1)).

It is conceivable that this right could be satisfied in a national context by an unfair competition approach,[65] but the Directive clearly aims at the creation of a sui generis right. The right subsists for 15 years from the completion of the making of the database (Article 10), and is subject to permitted acts, which are analogous to 'fair dealing' exceptions to copyright (Article 9). The Directive

[61] L Kaye, 'The Proposed EU Directive for the Legal Protection of Databases: A Cornerstone of the Information Society?' (1995) 12 *European Intellectual Property Review* 585 at 585.

[62] At 19.

[63] Recital 17.

[64] Article 7(1). See also Recital 40: 'whereas such investment may consist in the deployment of financial resources and/or the expanding of time, effort and energy.'

[65] F Grosheide, 'Database Protection—the European Way', paper delivered to the Heart of America Intellectual Property Law Conference, Washington University School of Law, April 2001, at para 15.

also provides for somewhat narrower copyright protection of the structure of the database, which is only to apply where the structure is the author's 'own intellectual creation'. (Article 3).

Article 7(1) above does not define the meaning of 'substantial', but the Explanatory Memorandum states that 'no fixed limits can be placed in this Directive as to the volume of material which can be used.'[66] Extraction and/or re-utilisation of *insubstantial* parts of the database which conflict with a normal exploitation of that database, or which unreasonably prejudice the legitimate interests of the maker of the database are also prohibited (Article 7(5)).

An example of the operation of this right can be seen in *British Horseracing Board Ltd and Others v William Hill Organsiation Ltd.*,[67] in which the defendants re-used for commercial purposes horse-racing information provided by the claimants, who employed 80 people to produce and maintain that information. The claimants successfully maintained that such re-use of the information was a breach of its database right.

The database right subsists for a considerable period of time—15 years from the date of completion of the database, or if later, the first making available to the public, and this period begins anew each time there is a 'substantial change' in the database.[68] The Preamble indicates that even a 'substantial verification' of the database constitutes a 'substantial change.'[69]

Finally, the international co-ordination evident in the Information Society Directive is similarly evident in the Database Directive. Article 11(3) provides that although the database right can only be enjoyed by Community database owners, the Council may extend protection to third country owners on the basis of special agreements (only one such agreement has so far been reached, that with the UK on behalf of the Isle of Man).[70]

Enforcement—Directive 2004/48/EC

In April 2004 the European Parliament and the Council adopted Directive 2004/48/EC on the enforcement of intellectual property rights.[71] The Directive was adopted within a short space of time (compared to the Directives considered in chapter 2 above) from the original Commission Proposal of January 2003[72] and concerns the measures, procedures and remedies necessary to

[66] Proposal, note 51 above, at 52.

[67] Note 14 above. The case involved the English law corresponding to the Directive, namely the Copyright and Rights in Databases Regulations (SI 1997/3032) 1997.

[68] Article 10.

[69] Recital 55.

[70] OJ 2003 L 89/11 (Council Decision), OJ 2003 L89/12–15 (Agreement).

[71] OJ 2004 L157/45.

[72] COM(2003) 46.

ensure the enforcement of intellectual property rights. It applies to any infringement of such rights as provided for by Community law and/or by the national law of the Member State concerned.[73]

The Directive imposes a general obligation on Member States to provide enforcement measures which are fair, equitable, not unnecessarily complicated or costly, and which do not entail unreasonable time-limits or delays.[74] This general obligation is inspired by Article 41(2) of the TRIPs (Trade Related Aspects of Intellectual Property Rights) Agreement,[75] although, the Directive, unlike TRIPs, makes no provision for criminal penalties (because of questions surrounding the competence of the Community to include the same within internal market legislation).[76] In addition to the general obligation above, the Directive gives three powerful rights to intellectual property rights holders.

First, Article 7(1) provides measures for preserving evidence which will be novel for many Member States' legal systems. Where there is reasonable evidence to indicate infringement, preservation action can be taken, including the physical seizure of goods, the materials and implements used in the production and/or distribution of the goods and the documents relating thereto; those measures may be taken without the other party having been heard. Paragraph 2 lays down that such measures may be subject to the applicant lodging security intended to ensure compensation for any prejudice suffered by the defendant. Article 7 is modelled on provisions which have demonstrated their effectiveness in national contexts, in particular the United Kingdom's *Doorstep* order and the French *saisie-contrefaçon*.[77]

Second, Article 8 gives a right to information, also modelled on successful national law (Germany, Belgium, the Netherlands and Luxembourg).[78] Judges are given the power to order the disclosure of information relating to the origin and distribution networks of the goods or services which infringe intellectual property by the infringer and/or any other person found in possession of infringing goods on a commercial scale, found using infringing goods on a commercial scale, found to be providing on a commercial scale services used in infringing activities, or was indicated by any person referred to above as being involved in the distribution, manufacture or distribution of the goods or the provision of the services.

Third, Article 9 provides for provisional and precautionary measures. Member States are required to ensure that the judicial authorities may issue against the alleged infringer an interlocutory injunction intended to prevent

[73] Article 2.
[74] Article 3(1).
[75] See www.wto.org.
[76] Commission Press Release IP/04/540, 26 April 2004.
[77] COM(2003) 46 at 21.
[78] COM(2003) 46 at 21.

any imminent infringement of intellectual property, or to forbid the continuation of the alleged infringements of that property, or to make such continuation subject to the lodging of guarantees intended to ensure the compensation of the rightholder. Where infringement is on a commercial scale Member States have to ensure that, if the injured party demonstrates circumstances likely to endanger the recovery of damages, the judicial authorities may order the precautionary seizure of the movable and immovable property of the alleged infringer, including the blocking of bank accounts and other assets. The latter right is inspired by the 'freezing order' long used in English law (previously 'Mareva injunction').

The above trio of rights—preservation, information, precaution—serves powerfully to ensure the enforcement of the authorship interests of producers.

Co-ordination

The Brussels Regulation 2000,[79] which largely supersedes the Brussels Convention 1968,[80] ensures that the rights provided for above are exercisable across Member States' borders. The Regulation provides that a person domiciled in one Member State may, in another Member State, be sued 'in matters relating to tort, delict or quasi-delict in the courts for the place where the harmful event occurred or may occur' (Article 5(3)). The European Court of Justice has never applied this provision or its identical predecessor to copyright or any related right. In the classic Internet infringement scenario of uploading content for free copying, the conception of the 'harmful event' might be restricted to the uploading. However, analogising from the case of *Shevill v Presse Alliance* discussed above,[81] it might be the case that foreign infringers are akin to those who damage reputation (as in *Shevill*) and thus susceptible to suit both in the jurisdiction of their domicile and the jurisdictions in which the relevant intellectual property right exists, which will usually in practice mean all Member States. The harmful event might in such a case be considered to be the damage to the 'right' itself, ie supplying the content for free copying in the jurisdiction which supports the property right.[82]

If the former analysis is adopted, the Brussels Regulation might be considered capable of intimidating a 'consumer' who uses a Web-site to copy a work within the 'fair use' parameters of her national law, yet becomes subject to suit in the domicile of the claimant. The Regulation provides some protection in

[79] Chapter 2, note 107 above.

[80] The Convention will continue to govern relations between Denmark and other Member States.

[81] Chapter 3, note 96 above.

[82] J Fawcett and P Torremans, *Intellectual Property in Private International Law* (Oxford University Press, 1998) at 164–7.

cases such as that above in as much as it does not require foreign judgements to be recognised if such recognition would be contrary to public policy in the Member State in which recognition is sought (Article 34(1)), but it is not at all clear whether this would be of succour to a consumer faced with a law-suit in a foreign country.

The Community has not harmonised rules as to the law applicable to non-contractual obligations, although the Commission in 2002 published its *Proposal for a Regulation on the law applicable to non-contractual obligations* ('Rome II').[83] The general rule proposed in the field of intellectual property is to be found in Article 8:

> 'The law applicable to a non-contractual obligation arising from an infringement of an intellectual property right shall be the law of the country for which protection is sought.'

Observations

The Community can be seen to offer comprehensive protection to authorship interests in e-commerce. The Information Society Directive protects the core of authors' interests in granting to authors exclusive rights to reproduce, distribute and communicate to the public, their original work. The Directive is closely co-ordinated with corresponding international instruments, facilitating global protection, and manifests the Community's success in achieving compromise amongst Member States with divergent approaches to copyright law.

In fact, the Directive might be argued to pay insufficient regard to the rights of users, despite its assertion of the need to safeguard 'a fair balance of rights and interests' between rightholders and users.[84] In particular, the Directive fails to make mandatory more than a single exception to the reproduction right, despite the well-established nature of many other exceptions, and implements no broad principle of fair use.

In addition to the Information Society Directive, the Community has further protected authors' interests through the adoption of the Directive on conditional access services, the Database Directive (creating the first sui generis database right in the world), the Directive on Enforcement of Intellectual Property Rights, and the Brussels Regulation 2000.

Taken together, the above instruments offer comprehensive protection which contrasts sharply with the incomplete protection of consumers' interests detailed in chapters 2 to 4 above. It will now be assessed whether the same is true in relation to producers' domain-identity interests.

[83] COM(2003) 427.

[84] Recital 31.

6

Producers II—Domain-Identity Interest

Introduction—The Threat to Producers' Domain-Identity Interest

The threat posed to producers' domain-identity interest is a simple one—namely that others may register a domain name consisting principally of a given producer's identity or similar, with a view to selling it on, or denying it, to the producer. This activity is known as 'cybersquatting' (or 'typosquatting' in cases where a slightly misspelt domain-name is registered). A registrant may deny such a domain name to a producer for the purpose of simply blocking consumers' online access to a competitor, or may be used in conjunction with a divert function to transfer consumers to a competitor site.

As pointed out in chapter 1 above, domain names are unique,[1] and thus cybersquatting a domain name excludes all others from it. A good example of the type of scavenging involved in cybersquatting is provided by the facts of the English case of *BT v One in a Million*,[2] in which the court held that the

[1] See pages 11–12 above.
[2] *BT and another v One in a Million Ltd. and others and other actions* [1998] 4 All ER 476.

defendants registered domain names containing trademarks with no intention other than selling them to the trademark owners. The claimants successfully sued for a preliminary injunction to stop the defendants contravening s10(3) of the Trade Marks Act 1994.

Self-help as a Solution?—The ICANN Process

The problem described above has to some extent been dealt with by a public/private hybrid form of regulation instituted by the organisation responsible for the Internet's addressing system, Internet Corporation for Assigned Names and Numbers ('ICANN').[3] It has created a process—the Uniform Dispute Resolution Process ('the Process')—designed to deal with the problem outlined above in as much as it afflicts generic top level domains.[4] The Process derives its force from the contract between the registrar and the registrant—all contracts for generic top level domain names provide for compulsory submission by the registrant to the Process in the event of a dispute over the use of a trade mark or service mark (a further 'public' aspect of the Process) in a domain name.[5]

History of the Process

The beginnings of the Process lie in a 1998 White Paper of the US Department of Commerce which called on the World Intellectual Property Organisation ('WIPO') to,

> 'initiate a balanced and transparent process, which includes the participation of trademark holders and members of the Internet community who are not trademark holders, to (1) develop recommendations for a uniform approach to resolving trademark/domain name disputes involving cyber-piracy (as opposed to conflicts between trademark holders with reasonable competing rights), (2) recommend a process for protecting famous trademarks in the generic top level domain, and (3) evaluate the effects . . . of adding new gTLDs and related dispute resolution procedures on trademark and intellectual property holders.'[6]

[3] www.icann.org.

[4] Ie .aero, .biz, .com, .coop, .info, .museum, .name, .net, and .org.

[5] For an example of a relevant contract, see http://www.networksolutions.com/legal/service-agreement.html.

[6] *Statement of Policy on Management of Internet Names and Addresses* (www.ntia.doc.gov/ntiahome/domainname/6_5_98dns.htm, 5 June 1998). See also gTLD Memorandum of Understanding, at www.itu.int/net-itu/gtld-mou/simple.htm and signatures to it at . . . mou/declare.htm.

The White Paper was not universally popular, WIPO was criticised as an inappropriate body to suggest solutions, being perceived in some quarters as biased in favour of trademark owners and against domain-name owners who had no corresponding trademark.[7] However, WIPO agreed to the task and settled its terms of reference as: making recommendations on dispute prevention, dispute resolution, protecting well-known marks in Global Top Level Domains and the potential effects on existing intellectual property of creating new Top Level Domain Names (such as .firm, .store etc). The work was generally characterised by *efforts* towards transparency and inclusivity: all relevant documents were made available on WIPO's Web-site, including the first draft terms of reference and the public's comments thereon;[8] an Expert Advisory Group, representative of diverse interests,[9] was established; open meetings were held in eleven cities around the world,[10] and their proceedings posted as audio files on WIPO's Web-site (reports were typically produced in English, French and Spanish).[11]

There were criticisms of the above-noted efforts towards inclusivity and transparency, including that many of the meetings were publicised less than three weeks ahead, and through little more than WIPO's own mailing lists, and that the drafting process itself was private.[12] The closed nature of WIPO's decision-making process contrasts unfavourably with the relatively open drafting undertaken for example by the Internet Engineering Task Force, which allows observers entry to all its meetings.

The Final Report of the WIPO Internet Domain Name Process—'The Management of Internet Names and Addresses: Intellectual Property Issues'—was adopted by the WIPO secretariat in April 1999 (it was never put to the WIPO General Assembly—the participation of the Member States of WIPO was limited to authorising the Secretariat to proceed (on 15 September 1998)).[13] This was duly taken up by ICANN, with one major exclusion, namely WIPO's recommendation to create *ex ante* global domain protection system for what it described as 'famous marks'.[14] The ICANN Domain Name Process

[7] See, for example, comments of K Kleiman and all on Request for Comment 1 (http://wipo2.wipo.int/dns_comments/0055.html, August 1998).

[8] Available at: http://wipo2.wipo.int/process/eng/rfc.html.

[9] Including trademark holders, technology, the registries, and (at a later stage) the public.

[10] Palo Alto, Washington DC, Mexico City, Asunción, Cairo, Hydrebad, Budapest, Brussels, Cape Town, Tokyo and Sydney.

[11] http://wipo2.wipo.int/process.eng/consult.html.

[12] M Froomkin, *Semi-Private International Rulemaking: Lessons Learned from the WIPO Domain Name Process* (www.law.miami.edu/~froomkin/articles/tprc99.htm, 1999) at 14–18 (Professor Froomkin was a member of WIPO's Expert Advisory Group).

[13] http://wipo2.wipo.int/process/eng/final_report.html. A second process began in June 2000, to resolve certain outstanding issues, completed in September 2001, see www.wipo.int.

[14] See generally, M Mueller, 'Technology and Institutional Innovation: Internet Domain Names' (2000) 5 *International Journal of Communications Law & Policy*, www.ijclp.org.

came into force on 1 December 1999,[15] and the first case was filed on 2 December 1999.[16]

The Process Rules and their Application

The Process requires registrants to submit to mandatory administrative proceedings in the event that a complainant third party asserts to the applicable Provider that:

> (i) [the] domain name is identical or confusingly similar to a trademark or service mark[[17]] in which the complainant has rights; and
> (ii) [the registrant has] no rights or reasonable interests in respect of the domain name; and
> (iii) [the] domain name has been registered and is being used in bad faith.[18]

The first paragraph above is self-explanatory. The second paragraph is further expanded upon within the Policy, stating that registrants have rights or reasonable interests in the domain name if they can demonstrate that: they used or were preparing to use the domain name in the bona fide offering of goods or services; or that they have been commonly known by the domain name; or that they are making a legitimate non-commercial or fair use of the domain name, without intent for commercial gain to misleadingly divert consumers or to tarnish the trademark or service mark at issue.[19]

As regards the third paragraph, the following is stated to be evidence of registration and use in bad faith:

> (i) circumstances indicating that you [the registrant] have registered or you have acquired the domain name primarily for the purpose of selling, renting, or otherwise transferring the domain name registration to the complainant who is the owner of the trademark or service mark or to a competitor of that complainant, for valuable consideration; or
> (ii) you have registered the domain name in order to prevent the owner of the trade mark or service mark from reflecting the mark in a corresponding domain name, provided you have engaged in a pattern of such conduct; or
> (iii) you have registered the domain name primarily for the purpose of disrupting the business of a competitor; or
> (iv) by using the domain name, you have intentionally attempted to attract, for commercial gain, Internet users to your web site or other online location, by

[15] www.icann.org/dnso/wga-final-report.htm.

[16] It was filed with WIPO, then the only accredited dispute resolution service provider, www.wipo.int/eng/pressrel/1999/p200.htm.

[17] It has been suggested that the lack of protection of geographical indications is a flaw in the ICANN Process, and indeed, it would seem arguable the identity interests of producers includes a collective interest in unique geographical identifiers. Work is ongoing on this problem, see http://wipo2.wipo.int/process2/index.html.

[18] Section 4(a).

[19] Section 4(c).

creating a likelihood of confusion with the complainant's mark as to the source, sponsorship, affiliation, or endorsement of your web site or location or of a product or service on your web site or location.[20]

The approach of Panels to the question of bad faith has been variable; however, five circumstances in particular have come to be routinely regarded as indicating bad faith.[21] First, non-use of a domain name (WIPO/D2000–0003, *telstra.org*); in *Telstra*, the Panel could not conceive of any possible legitimate interest that the respondent could make of the domain. In the later case of *jackspade.com* (WIPO/D2001–1384), the Panel held that the registrant's failure to use a domain containing a trade mark for three years shifted the burden of proof of a legitimate interest to the registrant, which it was in the event unable to satisfy.[22]

The second circumstance routinely regarded as indicating bad faith is where the registrant provides false contact information, or none. In various cases the Respondent has hidden its identity by using different names and the same post office address,[23] by giving a false telephone number,[24] and by providing incomplete information in the *WHOIS* directory.[25]

The third situation routinely regarded as indicating bad faith is where the registrant has a history of registering and then selling marks. Thus a NAF Panel has held that 'registration of a well-known trademark by a party with no connection to the owner of the trademark and no authorization and no legitimate purpose to utilize the mark reveals bad faith'.[26] Similarly, where a mark is not necessarily well-known, but merely known to the registrant, Panels have found registration to be evidence of bad faith where there is an absence of other legitimation: in one case the domain *fibershield.com* was registered further to a failed attempt to register *fiber-shield.com*;[27] in another the registrant knew of the trademark through a long history of competition.[28]

The fourth ground of evidence of bad faith is external linking. This might consist of automatic diverting to the Web-site of a competitor,[29] linking to such a Web-site,[30] or linking to a porn site.[31]

The fifth and final circumstance routinely regarded as indicating bad faith is that of 'typosquatting'. This has included multiple misspellings (eddiebau-

[20] Para 4(b).
[21] A Bender, 'Bad Faith', http://cyber.law.harvard.edu/udrp/opinion/btext.html (2002).
[22] See also NAF/FA94364 (dagmedia.com).
[23] WIPO/D2000–0501 (huntonwilliams.com).
[24] NAF/FA95345 (mediaenforcer.com).
[25] NAF/FA92016 (xtra.net).
[26] NAF/FA95314 (thecaravanclub.com).
[27] NAF/FA92054.
[28] WIPO/D2000–0139.
[29] WIPO/D2000–0861 (blackwaterrafting.com).
[30] WIPO/D2000–0037 (zwackunicum.com).
[31] NAF/FA95343 (simpleshoe.com).

rer.com and eddiebaur.com rather than eddiebauer.com),[32] as well as single (ggoogle.com instead of google.com,[33] plaboy.com instead of playboy.com).[34]

Panels have generally *declined* to find bad faith where the registrant registered the domain before the complainant registered any related trade mark (in *usource.com*[35] the registrant was not a competitor of the Complainant and registered the domain name five months before it was trade marked), and where a domain name is based on a generic word or words (eg *concierge.com*).[36]

Various cases have shown that it is possible for the requirement that the complainant have a trade mark or services mark can be satisfied by unregistered marks. For example in *Jeanette Winterson v Mark Hogarth*[37] the Complainant successfully asserted common-law trade mark rights in her name and obtained jeanettewinterson.com and related domain names from the defendant. Another example of protection of an unregistered mark occurred in *Cedar Trade Associates Inc. v Greg Ricks*,[38] in which the Complainant successfully asserted common law rights in 'BuyPC.com', which it had used as a trade name for the resale of personal computers and peripherals in the California area since January 1996. The Panel found that the Complainant had invested considerable effort in establishing an association between 'BuyPC.com' and its goods and services over approximately 4 years. The Panel's Decision accepted that it qualified as a trademark for the purposes of the Policy.

It is clear that a defendant cannot claim it has rights or reasonable interests in the domain name within the meaning of s4(a)(iii) above merely by virtue of having a vague plan to develop the site.[39]

Complainants may choose between any one of four accredited providers of arbitration panels to resolve their dispute:[40]

— Asian Domain Name Dispute Resolution Centre,[41]
— CPR Institute for Dispute Resolution,[42]
— The National Arbitration Forum [NAF],[43]
— World Intellectual Property Organisation [WIPO].[44]

32 WIPO/D2001–0224.
33 WIPO/D2001–0061.
34 WIPO/D2001–0094.
35 NAF/FA93533.
36 NAF/FA93547.
37 Case No. D2000–0235, http://arbiter.wipo.int/domains/decisions/html/2000/d2000–0235.html, 22 May 2000.
38 www.arbforum.com, File No. FA 0002 000093633, 25 February 2000.
39 See *Jeanette Winterson v Mark Hogarth*, note 37 above, at para 6.16.
40 http://www.icann.org/udrp/approved-providers.htm.
41 www.adndrc.org.
42 www.cpradr.org.
43 www.arbforum.com.
44 http://arbiter.wipo.int/domains/.

The decision of the arbitration panel is binding, subject to the defendant pursuing his or her case in a court of competent jurisdiction, and the complainant submitting to the jurisdiction of that court.[45]

On balance it can be seen that the Process rules are flexible in their content and application, and serve broadly to protect producers' domain-identity interest, as can be seen from the results shown in Table 1 below.[46]

TABLE 1: *ICANN Process as at August 2003*

Proceedings	Names	Proceeding Status
490	624	Pending
24	34	Case suspended at complainant's request
26	34	Case suspended, other
540	692	Total undisposed proceedings
5790	9941	Name transfer
46	59	Registration cancelled
1417	1825	Decision for respondent
56	629	Split decision
7309	12454	Dispositions by decision
8	15	Settlement with transfer
20	20	Settlement, unspecific result
7	10	Dismissal with prejudice
651	956	Dismissal without prejudice
200	266	Dismissal, unspecified
886	1267	Dispositions without decision
13	18	Proceedings terminated for recommencement

[45] The relevant provision is Article 4(k): 'the mandatory administrative proceeding requirements set forth in Paragraph 4 shall not prevent either you or the complainant from submitting the dispute to a court of competent jurisdiction for independent resolution before such mandatory administrative proceeding is commenced or after such proceeding is concluded. If an Administrative Panel decides that your domain name registration should be cancelled or transferred, we will wait ten (10) business days (as observed in the location of our principal office) after we are informed by the applicable Provider of the Administrative Panel's decision before implementing that decision. We will then implement the decision unless we have received from you during that ten (10) business day period official documentation (such as a copy of a complaint, file-stamped by the clerk of the court) that you have commenced a lawsuit against the complainant in a jurisdiction to which the complainant has submitted under Paragraph 3(b)(xiii) of the Rules of Procedure. (In general, that jurisdiction is either the location of our principal office or of your address as shown in our Whois database. See Paragraphs 1 and 3(b)(xiii) of the Rules of Procedure for details.) If we receive such documentation within the ten (10) business day period, we will not implement the Administrative Panel's decision, and we will take no further action, until we receive (i) evidence satisfactory to us of a resolution between the parties; (ii) evidence satisfactory to us that your lawsuit has been dismissed or withdrawn; or (iii) a copy of an order from such court dismissing your lawsuit or ordering that you do not have the right to continue to use your domain name.'

[46] http://www.icann.org/udrp/proceedings-stat.htm. See generally, S Jones, 'A Child's First Steps: The First Six Months of Operation—the ICANN Dispute Resolution Procedure for Bad Faith Registration of Domain Names' (2001) 23(2) *European Intellectual Property Review* 66.

In addition to the statistics detailed above, many illegitimate registrations which would have gone ahead in the absence of the Process have doubtless been forestalled.

Problems with the Process

Although the Process does offer broad protection for Community producers' identity interests, it is problematic in some respects. First, it is US-oriented. The ICANN-approved dispute resolution service providers display a marked US bias. A study in 2000 showed the following:

— **CPR:** 28 of CPR's 31 panel members were based in United States.
— **NAF:** All of its 61 panellists were retired US judges.
— **Disputes.org/eresolution:** 57 per cent of its panellists were based in the US (and many of the others were from common-law jurisdictions).
— **WIPO:** 25 per cent of the panellists were US-based.[47]

This bias creates the risk that US interests will be favoured in cases involving the same. Rule 15 of the Process provides that in reaching its decision the Panel may take into account 'any rules and principles of law it deems applicable', and indeed, in the first decision reached under the Policy, *World Wrestling Federation Inc v Michael Bosman*[48] the arbitrator looked only to US law in deciding the issue of whether offering a domain name for sale is 'use' within the meaning of Rule 4(a)(iii) of the Process.

A second danger arises from the fact that ICANN itself is located in California and thus ultimately subject to the jurisdiction of Californian and United States courts. This creates the danger that EU producers will be prejudiced by a claimant suing under US trademark law, and then seeking to force ICANN to implement any resulting ruling. This would not appear to have happened yet, but given the strong protection afforded to trademark interests in the US,[49] it would appear a real danger.

A third problem with the Process is its lack of independence. It is the *complainant* who selects the dispute resolution service provider (Article 4(d)

[47] As at 31 March 2000, *per* A Clark, 'Governance and Dispute Resolution in Cyberspace: Trade Marks *v* Domain Names', conference paper delivered at conference of the British and Irish Legal Educational Technology Association, April 2000. (The CPR figures were taken from www.cpr/org on 26 July 2000.)

[48] (WIPO Case No. D99–001 http://arbiter.wipo.int/domains/index.html). Offering for sale was found to be use, relying on the cases *Panavision International LP v Dennis Toeppen* (141 F 3d 1316 (9th Cir 1998)) and *Intermatic Inc. v Toeppen* (947 F Supp. 1227 (ND Ill. 1996)). See generally, C Waelde, 'Trade Marks and Domain Names: There's a Lot in a Name', in L Edwards and C Waelde (eds), *Law and the Internet* (Oxford, Hart Publishing, 2000).

[49] See in particular the Anticybersquatting Consumer Protection Act 1999 HR 3028 of October 26 1999, 15 USC.

UDRP: 'the complainant shall select the Provider from among those approved by ICANN by submitting the complaint to that Provider'), and this creates a danger that dispute resolution service providers will try to attract business by favouring complainants. Whilst other, more positive factors of competition exist (such as cost and speed), there is evidence that the above danger is manifesting itself—whilst WIPO received 29 per cent of filings in January 2000, that proportion rose to 61 per cent in July 2000, and at least one author has linked that substantial increase with WIPO's benevolence to claimaints.[50]

The fourth problem with the Process is that whilst it is essential for the confidence of all economic actors that the rules of the Process, once established, are adhered to, this has not always been the case.[51] Two examples are given below.

Dodgeviper.com[52]

This domain name was held from 1996 until 2000 by a fan of the Dodge Vipers. In 2000 the Dodge Vipers brought a claim and the single panellist found in the claimants' favour. In view of the fact that the site in question was clearly a fan site, and did not hold itself out as an official site, the decision that the fan had no 'reasonable interest' in the domain name (Process Rules, s.4(a)(ii)) does not seem to accord with ICANN's stated policy.

Catmachines.com[53]

This domain name was taken from the defendants, *Roam the Planet*, and awarded to the claimants, *Caterpillar*, on the basis that 'catmachines' is confusingly similar to *Caterpillar's* registered trademarks of 'cat' and 'caterpillar'. However, it can be argued that the two sets of word-strings are not confusingly similar at all. In particular, a consumer searching for Caterpillar on the Web would typically search for that very word, or its shortened version, 'cat', and not come across *catmachines.com* at all. Second, as the defendants pleaded, they did have an interest in the name unrelated to that of the claimants, in relation to Computer Aided Technology machines.

Such failures to adhere to the rules of the Process are exacerbated by the lack of any possibility to appeal directly from an administrative decision (although

[50] See M Geist, 'WIPO Wipes Out Domain Name Rights' (24/8/00) *The Globe and Mail* 9.

[51] See generally: C Oppedahl, 'Recent trademark cases examine reverse domain name hijacking' (1999) 21 *Hastings Communications & Entertainment Law Journal* 535; M Geist, *Fair.com? An Examination of the Allegations of Systematic Unfairness in the ICANN UDRP* (www.lawbytes.com, August 2001).

[52] Arbiter.wipo.int/domains/decisions/html/d2000–0222.html.

[53] Arbiter.wipo.int/domains/decisions/html/d2000–0275.html.

the defendant may be able to halt the implementation of the decision through court proceedings, as discussed below).

The fifth problem with the Process is that it is not usually applied to country-code domain names such as '.uk', and '.fr'. Thus it offers no succour for example to 'X' in the UK wanting to expand into France through the domain 'X.fr', only to find that the domain has been registered by a cybersquatter.

Although it has been suggested that the Process favours trade mark interests over other commercial identity interests,[54] this cannot itself be considered a serious problem for producers' identity interests given that these interests are virtually always protected by a trade mark. The Process has succeeded in neutralising part of the threat to producers' legitimate domain-identity interests; it is clearly rapid and effective, and in many cases litigants have used it in preference to the public courts.[55] However, it is not a perfect system, and it leaves a role for the Community in providing a fall-back for producers who gain no satisfaction from it.

Community Regulation

Supporting Self-help

The Community played an active role in the development of the WIPO and ICANN Processes described above,[56] and is currently a member of ICANN's Governmental Advisory Committee,[57] and was one of the twelve signatories to the request which provided the initial impetus to the second WIPO Process.[58] Further, the Commission has suggested that ICANN be placed under

[54] J Clausing, 'Trade Mark Holders Dominate', *New York Times*, 19 May 2000, http://www.nytimes.com/library/tech/00/05/cyber/cyberlaw/19law.html.

[55] Eg the first case filed, by the World Wrestling Federation, which could instead have used the United States' Anticybersquatting Consumer Protection Act 1999, 15 USC, section 1125(d)), given satisfaction of the issue of jurisdiction (which would not have been guaranteed however, see *AOL v Huang*, 2000 WL 991587 (EDVa) where the federal District Court in Virginia refused to assert jurisdiction over the defendant company on the mere basis that it had registered a Web address with Network Solutions, headquartered in Virginia). The Act concerns causes of action of infringement and dilution. It allows *in rem* actions against domain names: *Caesar's Palace Inc. v Caesars Palace.com*, EDVa, No. 99–550–A, 3 March 2000.

[56] See generally Commission, *Communication on Internet Governance: Management of Internet Names and Addresses*, COM(1998) 476. See also: High Level Report on the Information Society, *Recommendations to the European Council: Europe and the Global Information Society, (the 'Bangemann Report')*, (http://www.egd.igd.fhg.de:10555/WISE/globals/ecinfo/, 1994); K Essick, *European Commission wants minor role in Internet* (23 July 1998, The Industry Standard, http://www.thestandard.net/articles/news_display/0,1270,15155,00.html).

[57] http://www.noie.gov.au/projects/international/DNS/gac/library/meetings/gac1min.htm.

[58] http://wipo2.wipo.int/process2/rfc/letter2.html.

international control,[59] which might help to resolve the problems related to the US-bias of ICANN as described above. The suggestion, which has been echoed by the United Nations,[60] has not produced any positive response from the US or ICANN.

In addition to the above support for self-help, the Community has in place a substantial framework of trade mark law which serves to protect producers' identity interests, and which will now be discussed.

Substantive Protection

The Community has provided substantive protection of producers' domain-identity interest through the Trademark Directive of 1989[61] and the Trademark Regulation of 1994[62] (in conjunction with Directive 2004/48 on enforcement).[63] In accordance with Article 251 EC, the Directive *harmonised* various aspects of *national* trade mark laws. It is consistent with the Paris Convention for the Protection of Industrial Property (The 'Paris Convention'). The Regulation, consistent with the Paris Convention and the WTO TRIPs Agreement,[64] instituted a *directly applicable* Community trade mark system, enabling producers to achieve protection for a particular trade mark through a single registration.[65] The Regulation does not replace Member States' laws on trade marks, nor does it require undertakings to apply for registration of their trade marks as Community trade marks. The Directive and the Regulation are discussed separately below.

The Trade Mark Directive

The Trade Mark Directive provides that a trade mark may consist of,

> 'any sign capable of being represented graphically, particularly words, including personal names, designs, letters, numerals, the shape of goods or of their packaging, provided that such signs are capable of distinguishing the goods or services of one undertaking from those of other undertakings.' (Article 2).

[59] Commission, *The Organisation and Management of the Internet—International and European Policy Issues 1998–2000*, COM(2000) 202.

[60] See www.unicttaskforce.org/.

[61] Directive 89/104/EEC, OJ 1989 L40/1. See generally on trade mark protection in e-commerce: Commission, *Globalisation and the Information Society, The Need for Strengthened International Co-ordination*, COM(98)50; Commission, *Issues Involving the Registration of Domain Names*, (www.ispo.cec.be/, July 1997).

[62] Council Regulation 40/94 on the Community trade mark, OJ 1994 L11/1, as amended by Regulation 3288/94, OJ 1994 L349/83.

[63] Discussed at p 108 and following above.

[64] Recitals 2 and 3.

[65] Article 2. Registration takes place at the Office for the Harmonisation of the Internal Market in Alicante.

The definition above clearly covers the word-strings which make up domain names. Trade mark owners are entitled to prevent all third parties from using in the course of trade:

> '(a) any sign which is identical with the trade mark in relation to goods or services which are identical with those for which the trade mark is registered;
> (b) any sign where, because of its identity with, or similarity to, the trade mark and the identity or similarity of the goods or services covered by the trade mark and the sign, there exists a likelihood of confusion on the part of the public, which includes the likelihood of association between the sign and the mark.' (Article 5).

It is clear that Article 5(a) covers the typical cybersquatting case (the question of 'use' will be discussed in the following section), as has been held by a number of national courts considering corresponding national provisions.[66] Further, the Directive supports participation in the ICANN Process by ensuring that producers can rely on a trade mark, which is a necessary constituent of a complainant's claim under the Process as described above.

The Community Trade Mark Regulation[67]

> 'Whereas it is desirable to promote throughout the Community a harmonious development of economic activities . . . legal conditions must be created which enable undertakings to adapt their activities to the scale of the Community . . . [T]rade marks enabling the products and services of undertakings to be distinguished by identical means throughout the Community, regardless of frontiers, should feature amongst the instruments which undertakings have at their disposal.' (Recital 1).

The basic qualifying criteria for registration of a Community Trade Mark are set out in Article 4, and are the same as those in Article 2 of the Directive, quoted above. Not all signs can be registered, in particular those for which an earlier trade mark has been registered in a Member State.[68] If a sign is accepted for registration, the Regulation provides that its owner shall be entitled to prevent all third parties not having his consent from using in the course of trade:

> '(a) any identical sign in relation to goods or services which are identical with those for which the Community trade mark is registered,
> (b) any identical or similar sign used in relation to goods or services identical or similar to those for which the Community trademark is registered, where there is a likelihood of confusion on the part of the public,

[66] See eg *BT v One in a Million*, note 2 above (although note that the decision in that case was principally driven by the common law relating to passing off).
[67] Note 62 above.
[68] Article 8.

> (c) any identical or similar sign *not* used in relation to goods or services identical or similar to those for which the Community trademark is registered, but where the latter has a reputation in the Community[69] and where use of that sign without due cause takes unfair advantage of, or is detrimental to, the distinctive character or the repute of the mark.' (Article 9(1)).

Whilst it might be argued that cybersquatters are not 'using' a sign in simply holding a related domain name for sale or otherwise passively, such can be considered 'use' in as much as such holding is positive action; this has been the conclusion of several national courts in considering parallel national provisions.[70] The above analysis is buttressed by Article (2)(b) of the Regulation, which prohibits the stocking of goods under a sign identical or similar to a trade mark for the purpose of offering them for sale, ie for the Regulation to bite it is not necessary to sell or offer for sale.[71] Cybersquatting certainly contravenes the first limb of Article 9(1)(c) above and probably also the second—cybersquatting clearly takes unfair advantage of the distinctive character of trade marks in seeking to profit from the investment of the owner; it is also arguably detrimental to the distinctive character and repute of a mark in as much as modern consumers might be said to expect, for their own convenience, that trade marks will be directly linked to domain names.

The strength of protection offered by Article 9(1)(c) is partly dependent upon the meaning ascribed to the term 'reputation', the wider the meaning the stronger the protection, the ECJ has made clear in the case of *Canon Kabushiki Kaisha v Metro-Goldwyn-Mayer Inc.*[72] that the term is to be interpreted widely. In that case, the Court denied the defendants' attempt to register *Cannon* as a trade mark for motion pictures and related services, holding that it would dilute the claimants' 'Canon' trade mark, held for photographic devices, stating:

> 'Marks with a highly distinctive character, either per se or because of the reputation they possess on the market, enjoy broader protection than marks with a less distinctive character.'[73]

Indeed it has been argued that producers only have to establish that their mark is exclusively associated with their goods or services in order to establish a 'reputation'.[74]

Thus it can be seen that the Regulation allows producers to pre-empt speculative cross-border cybersquatting within Europe—eg Producer X in the UK

[69] The meaning of this phrase is discussed below.

[70] See eg *BT v One in a Million* (in the UK), note 2 above, and *Panavision v Toeppen* (in the US), note 48 above.

[71] Article 9(2)(b).

[72] Case C–39/97, [1999] 1 CMLR 77.

[73] At para 18.

[74] F Mostert, *Famous and Well Known Marks* (London, Butterworths, 1997) at 23.

can register 'X' as a Community trade mark and thus severely limit the possibilities for cybersquatters to profit from registering X.fr, X.it etc.

The '.eu' Top Level Domain

The Commission in 2000 published a *Proposal for a Regulation of the European Parliament and of the Council on the implementation of the Internet Top Level Domain* '.eu',[75] having first mooted the idea in 1999.[76] The Proposal was adopted in April 2002 as Regulation 733/2002.[77] The objective of Regulation 733/2002 is to further the implementation of the .eu country code top level domain within the Community. It designates a Registry, now established as the European Registry for Internet Domain names ('EURid'),[78] a non-profit organisation based in Brussels and formed under Belgian law.

EURid is obliged under the Regulation to implement an

> 'extra-judicial settlement of conflicts policy . . . to resolve promptly disputes between domain name holders regarding rights relating to names including intellectual property rights . . . [T]his policy shall . . . take into consideration the recommendations of the World Intellectual Property Organisation . . .' (Article 4(2)(d)).

It is further provided in Article 5(1)(a) of the Regulation that the Commission shall adopt public policy rules on

> 'speculative and abusive registration of domain names including the possibility of registrations of domain names in a phased manner to ensure appropriate temporary opportunities for the holders of prior rights recognised or established by national and/or Community law . . .'

Those rules have now been adopted through *Commission Regulation (EC) 874/2004 laying down public policy rules concerning the implementation and functions of the .eu Top Level Domain and the principles governing registration.*[79]

As at July 2004 EURid is not operational. Its Web-site then gave the following answer to the Frequently Asked Question 'When will EURid become operational?'

> '— We cannot begin .eu registrations at this time or set a definitive date to commence.
> — We are in the final stages of contractual negotiations with the European Commission.

[75] COM(2000) 827. The progress of the '.eu' project can be followed at: http://europa.eu.int/ISPO/eif/InternetPoliciesSite/DotEU/WorkD ocEN.html.

[76] Commission, *eEurope An Information Society for All*, COM(1999) 812, at 9.

[77] OJ 2002 L113/1. The Regulation use of '.eu' is in line with the IANA's policy of using the International Standards Organisation's 2-letter country code indicators as top level domains (ISO3166), see http://www.iana.org/cctld/cctld.htm and www.iso.ch.

[78] www.eurid.org.

[79] OJ (2004) L162/40.

— We must then make an agreement with ICANN and have .eu TLD put into the root.
— When contractual negotiations are completed, we will begin to accredit .eu registrars and publish a list on our web site.
— Those wanting a .eu domain name will need to contact one of these registrars.
— As soon as possible, we will publish full rules and procedures for .eu registrations including the Sunrise period. Until we receive the contract from the Commission we have printed a tentative timetable which expresses each event as time elapsed after the contract. When the contract is signed, we will announce actual dates.'

It is clear that the beginning of the '.eu' domain name is dependent upon two events, first the awarding of a contract by the Commission, and second the agreement of ICANN to adopt '.eu' as a top level domain. EURid has published a provisional timetable to be applied on the occurrence of the above two events,[80] set out in Table 2 below:

TABLE 2: *Provisional Timetable for EURid:*

Immediately upon contracts	Engage ADR suppliers and finalise ADR procedures.
Contracts + 1 month	Publish job descriptions & begin recruiting staff.
Contracts + 1 month	Publish proposed .eu Registration Policy —for comment.
Contracts + 1 month	Make available the terms and condition of registration in official EU languages—including ADR provisions.
Contracts + 6 weeks	Make available the registrar agreement in all official EU languages. Begin accrediting .eu registrars and publishing names on the web site.
Contracts + 4 months	Announce final Registration policy including Sunrise rules and procedures and widely announce Sunrise dates.
Contracts + 5 months	Make registration software available for registrar testing.
Contracts + 8/9 months	Start phase 1 of Sunrise (public bodies and holders of trademarks may apply for the corresponding name).
Start of sunrise + 2 months	Start phase 2 of Sunrise period (those eligible to apply in phase 1 plus holders of other rights recognised in the national law of a member state may apply for the corresponding name).
Start of sunrise + 4 months	Sunrise period closes and registrations open on a first-come-first-served basis. Validation of names applied for during Sunrise continues until task completed.

[80] http://eurid.org/Information/timetable.html.

Once, and if, operational, the '.eu' top level domain name will provide useful protection of producers' identity interests.

Co-ordination

The Community has acted to facilitate enforcement of the above rights across Member States' borders both through the adoption of the Brussels Regulation 2000[81] and through the Community trade mark courts. The Brussels Regulation provides that a person domiciled in one Member State may, in another Member State, be sued in matters relating to tort, delict or quasi-delict in the courts for the place where the harmful event occurred or may occur (Article 5(3)). Thus for example, if a Polish company tries to attract consumers looking for *Wilson* sports goods by registering the variation '*wilsons.fr*' in France, then given that the relevant trade mark is held in France, the holder does not have to sue in Poland but rather can sue in France, and can there doubtless obtain an order for the transfer of the domain name.

As regards Community trade marks, the Regulation prescribes that actions for infringement be pursued in the jurisdiction of the defendant's domicile,[82] heard by a Community trade mark court (albeit in substance a national court), applying the Regulation itself.[83]

The Community has not harmonised rules as to the law applicable to non-contractual obligations, although the Commission in 2002 published its *Proposal for a Regulation on the law applicable to non-contractual obligations* ('Rome II').[84] The general rule proposed in the field of intellectual property is to be found in Article 8:

> 'The law applicable to a non-contractual obligation arising from an infringement of an intellectual property right shall be the law of the country for which protection is sought.'

Observations

The Community can be seen closely to protect producers' domain-identity interest. The Trademark Directive ensures a minimum level of protection for producers, both through national courts and in conjunction with the ICANN Process. The Trademark Regulation largely negates the threat posed by

[81] Chapter 2 note 107 above.
[82] Trademark Regulation, Articles 90(a), 93; Brussels Regulation, Article 22(4).
[83] Article 97(1).
[84] COM(2003) 427.

cross-border cyber-squatting, and the Directive on IP Enforcement provides valuable rights within its sepcific sphere. The Community has further moved towards the adoption of a '.eu' top level domain with *ex ante* control of registrations containing trade marks.

As with authorship interests, the Community's protections of the domain-identity interest are tied into a broad international framework—the Trademark Directive and Regulation are co-ordinated with the Paris Convention for the Protection of Industrial Property and the WTO TRIPs Agreement. Finally, it can be pointed out that the Community played an active part in developing the ICANN Process.

7

Conclusions

The Imbalance Between the Protection of Consumers' and Producers' Critical Interests

This book has shown a sharp contrast between faltering protection of consumers' critical interests in e-commerce on the one hand, and near-comprehensive protection of producers' corresponding interests on the other. This contrast is summarised below.

Consumers' Fair Trading Interests

Protective aspects:
— rights to pre- and post-contract information, and to a mandatory cooling-off period (Directive on distance contracts).
— provision for Member States to encourage codes of conduct (Directives on e-commerce and on distance contracts).

— mandatory self-identification of commercial providers of information society services (Directive on e-commerce).
— a general capacity to sue in the country of domicile, and protection from suit elsewhere (Brussels Regulation on jurisdiction).

Gaps:
— restricted meaning of 'consumer' (Directives on e-commerce and on distance contracts).
— failure to reflect consumers' varying conceptions of 'fair' marketing practices (the home country control principle in the Directive on e-commerce).
— a pattern of inadequacy within the Directive on distance contracts, including failure to cover financial services (now remedied by the Directive on the distance marketing of financial services), to protect advance payments, to ensure that the consumer is aware of her right of withdrawal, and to ensure that consumers receive all requisite information.
— a generalised failure to provide an enforcement framework which reflects the diffuse nature of consumers' fair trading interest, in particular to make it worthwhile for individual consumers, or collectives of consumers, to pursue consumer rights (although there has been a *partial* attempt to deal with these problems in the Commission's Proposal for a Regulation on Consumer Protection Cooperation). Furthermore, the Community has failed to provide for easy access to a counter-party through manufacturer liability in respect of goods which do not conform to contract, arguably the key to generating consumer confidence in cross-border e-commerce.

Consumers' Privacy Interests

Protective aspects:
— a broad public law framework for the protection of consumers' privacy interests, including provisions on notice, consent, security and access (the Directives on privacy and on electronic privacy).

Gaps:
— a lack of clarity.
— a failure to ensure that consumers are given *meaningful* notice that their personal data will be collected.
— a failure to deal with the particular problems presented by children's privacy.
— a failure to provide a general enforcement framework which reflects the diffuse nature of impingements on consumers' privacy.
— a failure to ensure that the Directive is effective in the important forum of the United States, where the Safe Harbour Principles lack the teeth necessary to protect consumers' interests.

Consumers' Morality Interests

Protective aspects:
— a series of soft-law measures designed to support self-help initiatives.

Gaps:
— (given the admittedly difficult question of competence) a failure to take the minimum action of instituting a system of on-demand public rating by Member States of online content unsuitable for children.

Producers' Authorship Interests

Protective aspects:
— protection of authors' interests in controlling reproduction, distribution and communication to the public (the Information Society Directive).
— (novel) protection in respect of illicit re-use of original work (the Database Directive).
— protection from illicit access (the Directive on conditional access services).
— facilitation of the practical value of the above-mentioned rights through the Directive on IP Enforcement.
— facilitating the enforcement of these rights outside the Community through the reciprocity provisions of the Berne Convention.

Gaps:
— no major gaps.[1]

Producers' Domain-Identity Interest

Protective aspects:
— the Trade Mark Directive, providing a minimum level of protection, and supporting the position of producers within the ICANN Process.
— broad protection through the Community Trade Mark Regulation, the first non-national trade mark system in the world.
— movement towards a '.eu' top level domain name with *ex ante* protection for trade marks.
— facilitation of the enforcement of the above-mentioned rights within the Community through the Directive on IP enforcement and the Brussels Regulation.

Gaps:
— no major gaps.[2]

[1] A caveat is here necessary relating to the current levels of illegal copying amongst Internet users. However, most of this is not-for-profit and it might be expected to reduce somewhat when the Directive on IP Enforcement is implemented.

[2] Although trade mark owners might argue for legislation specifically directed against the activities of cybersquatters, similar to the Anti-Cybersquatting Consumer protection Act 1999 in the US, it would seem that the existing regime does largely protect producers' domain-identity interest.

Summary

Failings can be seen in all three consumer fields, while there are no serious gaps in the Community's protection of producers' interests. The most likely explanation of this imbalance would seem to be the diffusion of consumers' interests in comparison with those of producers. This comparative diffusion exists at national level, but is even greater at the Community level, where no uniform consumer identity exists. In contrast, producers often do have a discrete European identity in the form of an office, and also often act as organised lobbies. The diffusion of consumers' interests hinders lobbying . In particular, it can be argued that the costs to individual consumers of investing in representation of their interests generally outweigh the potential benefits, at least in the short-term.[3]

A further likely reason for the imbalance in the Community's approach to protecting producer and consumer interests is the secondary importance which the Community has historically attached to consumer protection.[4] Market integration is one of the driving forces of the Community, having been considered by the founders to be the best way to help Europe avoid repeating the mistakes of Second World War.[5] With its focus on market integration, the Community can be argued to have prioritised the free movement of goods and services over and above the protection of consumers, it being easier to reach political agreement on negative rules forbidding restrictions on the free movement of goods and services than on the technically complex positive rules required for consumer protection. Indeed it was not until 1987, thirty years after the establishment of the Community, that consumer protection was granted discrete status within the EC Treaty.[6] Yet ten years later Professor Stephen Weatherill felt able to comment, 'Although there is a collection of EC legal materials which affects the consumer, is it straining analytical coherence to describe this as a "consumer policy"?'[7]

[3] M Olson, *The Logic of Collective Action: Public Goods and the Theory of Groups* (Cambridge Mass., Harvard University Press, 1965) at 166 and following; See also R Winter, 'Economic Regulation vs Competition: Ralph Nader and Creeping Capitalism' (1973) 82 *Yale Law Journal* 890.

[4] See generally T Wilhelmsson, 'The Abuse of the 'Confident Consumer' as a Justification for EC Consumer Law' (2004) 27 *Journal of Consumer Policy* 317.

[5] See generally, D Urwin, *The Community of Europe: A History of European Integration since 1945* (London, Longman, 1996). (Fear of war was also of course the driving force behind the creation of the Internet. As noted in chapter 1 above, the Internet grew out of research into safeguarding the efficacy of US military computer networks.)

[6] Article 129a, inserted in the EC Treaty by the Single European Act, see generally on the history of consumer protection in the Community, N Reich, 'From contract to trade practices law: protection of consumers' economic interests by the EC', in T Wilhelmsson (ed), *Perspectives on Critical Contract Law* (Aldershot, Dartmouth, 1993).

[7] S Weatherill, *EC Consumer Law and Policy* (London, Longman, 1997) at 152.

The Community's failures might be mitigated in the future by technical changes to the architecture of the Internet, a topic which has attracted considerable comment from scholars.[8] In particular, a requirement of verified identity to set up a domain, Web-site or e-mail account may protect consumers from fraudsters. The top level domains, such as '.com' and '.org', might eventually be supplanted by mandatory country-code top level domains, which would diminish one aspect of the Net's borderlessness—although there are no current plans for such supplantation. Further, the computers attached to the Net may in the future have unique permanent identifiers that further reduce borderlessness and the anonymity of users.[9] Although the traditionally liberal character of the Net might militate against such developments, its increasingly commercial character militates in favour, as does the actual or perceived aid they might lend to national security.

As it currently stands, Community regulation is inadequate. The failure to protect consumers' critical interests does not bode well for the rapid development within the Community of a vibrant electronic marketplace (nor for e-commerce elsewhere, given the propensity of third countries to take Community law as a model).[10] Just as individuals across the world only belatedly appreciated the impact of the WTO Agreement and of the Community's food safety rules,[11] so the consequences of the Community's regulation of e-commerce may not become apparent for some years. Member States are engaged in an ongoing process of implementation, and the marketplace itself is constantly adapting to changes in technology and commercial habit.

[8] See for example: L Lessig, *Code is Law* (New York, Basic Books, 1999); J Reidenberg, 'Lex Informatica: The Formulation of Information Policy Rules Through Technology' (1998) 76(3) *Texas Law Review* 553; G Greenleaf, 'An Endnote on Regulating Cyberspace: Architecture v Law?' (1998) 21(2) *University of New South Wales Law Journal* 593.

[9] See generally: J Weinberg, 'Hardware-based ID, rights-management, and trusted systems', 21/08/99 www.law.wayne.edu/weinberg/; Patrick Gesinger (Intel), 'A Billion Trusted Computers', at RSA Data Security Conference 20 January 1999, available at www.intel.com/pressroom/archive/speeches/pg012099.htm.

[10] As an example of the extra-territorial influence of Community law, see the discussion of the Product Liability Directive in D Harland, 'Some Reflections on the influence outside Europe of the EC Directive on Product Liability', in L Kramer, H-W Micklitz and K Tonner (eds), *Law and Diffuse Interests in the European Legal Order* (Baden-Baden, Nomos, 1997).

[11] Both these sets of rules went unnoticed by most people at their formulation, yet in their impact damaged confidence in their respective institutions—as shown by the WTO—related riots in 1999 in Seattle, and the various recent food scandals within the Community.

Research Findings

Generalised Fault-lines—A Lack of Clarity and Slow Response-times

In addition to the Community's general failure to protect consumers' critical interests, the chapters above reveal two additional fault-lines in its regulation of e-commerce, a lack of clarity and a slow response-time. These will now be considered in turn.

(a) Lack of clarity

Community regulation of e-commerce is opaque, both in relation to its substance and to its processes. The many Community instruments affecting e-commerce are not easy to aggregate. The relevant Directives do not always autonomously define important terms which they contain; for example, Article 2(a) of the Directive on e-commerce (chapter 2 above), which defines 'information society service' as 'services within the meaning of Article 1(2) of Directive 98/34/EC as amended by Directive 98/48/EC'. Nor are the definitions used consistent; contrast for example the definition of 'consumer' in Directive 97/7 on distance contracts—'any natural person who . . . is acting for purposes which are outside his trade, business or profession', (Article 2(2))—with that in Directive 99/44 on guarantees—'any natural person who . . . is acting for purposes which are not related to his trade, business or profession', (Article 1(2)(a)).[12] Further, Directives are amended without any official consolidated version being produced. These problems will grow as the Community *acquis* itself grows. National governments are sometimes in a position to ameliorate these problems during transposition, but do not always do so.[13] Community legislation has built up to such an extent that some systemisation, perhaps in the form of a Code or Codes, would aid its comprehensibility; it should be emphasised that by 'Code' is here meant codifying existing law, rather than creating new law.[14] Indeed the construction of a *framework* code, to be developed as

[12] On a more positive note, as regards form if not substance, there does seem to have been some consistency recently, see Directive 2000/31 on e-commerce and Directive 2002/65 on the distance marketing of financial services, both of which follow Directive 99/44 above.

[13] For example, the UK government has been criticised for its tendency to simply 'copy-out' the contents of Directives, see eg S Bright and C Bright, 'Unfair Terms in Land Contracts: Copy Out or Cop Out?' (1995) 111 *Law Quarterly Review* 655. On a more positive note, the UK Government has recently announced an intention to standardise its implementations of the Community's varying definitions of 'consumer', see Department of Trade and Industry, *Consumer Guarantees: A Consultation Document* (http://www.dti.gov.uk/cacp/ca/consulta.htm, January 2001).

[14] The same suggestion has been made in relation to English consumer law: G Howells, 'A Consumer Code for the United Kingdom?' [1995] *Consumer Law Journal* 201. One might usefully compare the current inaccessibility of Community law with the German Civil Code, copies of which are widely available at German railway stations. Note should also be made here of the

necessary by the courts, has been suggested as the most appropriate way for the law to deal with the dynamic character of the Net.[15] Although it might be argued that a code would not improve the substance of the law, it would contribute to increased transparency, possibly stimulating greater coherence. A more coherent approach would give market actors greater confidence and enable courts across the Community more easily to give harmonious interpretations of the law. In Case C-96/95, *Commission v Germany* the ECJ stated that Member State implementation must,

> 'guarantee the full application of the directive in a sufficiently clear and precise manner so that, where the directive is intended to create rights for individuals, the persons concerned can ascertain the full extent of their rights . . .'[16]

Not only the substance but also the processes of Community law can be opaque. Chapter 2 above noted that the Commission pursued work on revising the Rome Convention on the Law Applicable to Contractual Obligations 1980, without engaging in any kind of public consultation. It has been seen in chapter 3 how certain Commission documents relating to US-EU negotiations on data protection were not made public by the Commission, but were available on the Web-site of the US Department of Commerce. More positively, it can be noted that although *drafts* of the Directive on e-commerce granted the Commission powers similar to those it holds under the Directive on data protection, those powers were omitted from the final version.[17] Also,

existence of various academic projects designed to test the feasibility of a *wider* European Civil Code, see in particular the Study Group on a European Civil Code (von Bar project), detailed at http://ecc.kub.nl/index.php3. See generally: A Hartkamp and all (eds), *Towards a European Civil Code* (Nijmegen, Ars Aequi Libris, 1998); R Zimmerman, 'Civil Code and Civil Law: The "Europeanisation" of Private Law Within the European Community and the Re-emergence of a European Legal Science' (1997) 6 *Columbia Journal of European Law* 63; P Legrand, 'Against a European Civil Code' (1997) 60 *Modern Law Review* 44.

[15] L Lessig, 'The Path of Cyberlaw' (1995) 104 *Yale Law Journal* 1743. Some of the problems with the substance of Community law may stem from the Community's law-making process, individual Directorates-General will generally be responsible for producing a first draft of proposals. This may gestate for some time before any other Directorate-General comes to know of its contents, or even its existence. See generally: N Nugent, *The Government and Politics of the European Union* (Basingstoke, Macmillan, 1994); M Raworth, *The Legislative Process in the European Community* (Deventer, Kluwer, 1993).

[16] [1997] ECR I–1653 at 1654.

[17] Under the Draft Directive (chapter 2 note 35 above), assisted by the Advisory Committee the Commission had the power to:

— decide on the compatibility of national derogations with Community law (subject of course to review by the European Court of Justice under Article 234 of the Treaty), Article 22(3)(d).
— make rules governing co-operation between national authorities in the supervision of information service providers, Article 19(6).
— stipulate the information which can be given by regulated professions (eg the medical and legal professions) for the purposes of providing information society services, Article 8(3).
— amending the list in Annex I of activities of Information Society services excluded from the Directive, Article 22(1)(c).

recent efforts by the Commission towards inclusivity can be identified in the hearings it conducted prior to the adoption of the Brussels Regulation 2000.[18]

(b) Slow response-times

The typical timescale of the Community Directives considered in this book is approximately two to three years from Proposal to Directive and then a further two or three years for national transposition. The process can take much longer: the Directive on Distance Contracts began as a Proposal in 1992, was adopted in 1997, and its due date for transposition was 2000—a total of eight years. Such a timescale is glacial in comparison to the rapid development of e-commerce, and can result in law which is out-of-date before it is due to be implemented. On the other hand, the deficiencies in the rapidly-adopted Directive on e-commerce might be attributed to the desire of politicians to be seen to be doing something in response to new problems—a balance clearly needs to be struck between rapid reaction and careful consideration.

A good example of how the law in this area can date quickly is to be found in Directive 95/46 on privacy—although adopted as recently as 1995, its reliance on the concept of a 'data controller' is more suited to the era of mainframes than distributed networks, as discussed in chapter 3 above.

In some areas, the Community does not compare well with the US, which for example legislated on intermediary liability for copyright infringement in 1998,[19] whilst the Community did not do so until 2000.[20] Slow Community action may have knock-on effects at national level, as initiatives there are put on hold awaiting resolution of the Community position.[21]

Community regulation is hampered not only by slow *law-making*, but also by slow and sometimes ineffective *law-enforcing*. Inadequate law-enforcement can result in consumers and producers being left in a worse position than having no legal protection at all, as Professor Udo Reifner has pointed out:

> 'It can even be argued that the more consumer protection appears on the statute book, the less practical means are offered to protect the interests of consumers in the marketplace—particularly where help and support is most needed.'[22]

[18] Chapter 2 note 107 above. A report from the hearing was available at www.europa.eu.int/comm/scic/conferences/991104/991104info.htm at November 2000, but has since been removed.

[19] The Digital Millennium Copyright Act 1998.

[20] With the adoption of the Directive 2001/31 on e-commerce (which had a further transposition period of two years).

[21] This has occurred recently for example in the field of sales law. A number of Scandinavian countries put relevant reforms on hold for some six or so years pending adoption of Directive 99/44/EC on Consumer Guarantees, see the Web-site of the Norwegian Ministry of Justice: www.odin.dep.no/jd/engelsk/index-b-n-a.html. (Norway is bound by the Directive as a member of the European Economic Area).

[22] 'The Future of Consumer Education and Consumer Information in a Market Economy', in T Wilhelmsson and all (eds), *Consumer Law in the Information Society* (Kluwer Law International, The Hague, 2001) 67 at 67.

The existence of law can distract attention from the fact that the underlying problem it seeks to resolve is ongoing—in particular law can provide a foil for those in favour of the status quo, who can demand 'time' for the law to work.

Ensuring timely transposition is the first stage in Community law-enforcing and a good example of inadequacy in that area can be found in relation to Directive 95/46 on Data Protection, which only four Member States managed to transpose on time.[23] The problem of slow transposition is endemic, Directive 94/47/EC on Timesharing for example was transposed on time by just two Member States.[24] This failure to recognise the importance of rapid action extends also to the European Court of Justice—Advocate General Tesauro once criticised the Commission as 'overhasty, to say the least' for bringing an action against a Member State for alleged mis-transposition of a Directive *eight years* after the relevant transposition! He argued that the Commission should have waited for a national test-case, a suspect argument given that a test-case might have taken an inordinately long time to materialise (consumer claims are often of such low value that they are uncommon in higher, reported courts, and producers may seek to preserve 'grey' law by settling cases before judgment).[25]

There are problems beyond transposition. A Directive that is transposed without resources being made available to support its effectiveness post-transposition, in terms of both educating economic actors and enforcement, may not be effective. Yet the Community does not have an adequate supervision system in place to ensure that transposed laws are effective in practice. Article 226 EC empowers the Commission to ensure Community law is properly observed yet the Commission only has the resources to check on correct transposition.[26] Further the Commission is not the impartial arbiter needed in the matter of checking on adequate enforcement. It is a political institution constantly involved in a wide-range of delicate negotiations with Member States. In mitigation, it can be said that individuals do benefit from certain controls on national breaches of Community law, including the doctrines of

[23] See D Korff, 'Study on Implementation of Data Protection Directive—Comparative Summary of National laws', May 2003, www.europa.eu.int/comm/internal_market/en/media/dataprot.

[24] *Per* Commission, Report on the Application of Directive 94/47/EC of the European Parliament and Council of 26 October 1994 on the protection of purchasers in respect of certain aspects of contracts relating to the purchase of the right to use immovable properties on a timeshare basis, (www.europa.eu.int/comm/dg24/policy/developments/timeshare/time02_en.html, 1999).

[25] Case C–300/95 *Commission v United Kingdom* [1997] ECR I–2649 at para 29 (the case concerned the Directive on Product Liability).

[26] See L Borzsak, 'Punishing Member States or Influencing Their Behaviour or *Iudex (non) calculat?*' (2001) 13 *Journal of Environmental Law* 235; R Mastroianni, 'The Enforcement Procedure under Article 169 of the EC Treaty and the powers of the European Commission: Quis Custodiet Custodes?' (1995) 1 *European Public Law* 535.

direct effect,[27] indirect effect,[28] and state liability.[29] However, the effectiveness of these controls is not comprehensive. Legislation may not meet the requisite criteria to be of direct effect—namely that it is sufficiently clear and unconditional to be justiciable. This was a problem for example in *El Corte Ingles SA v Christina Blasquez Rivera*, in which the Court refused to allow the defendant to rely directly on the provisions of Directive 87/102/EEC on consumer credit, then unimplemented in Spain.[30] All three of the above-mentioned controls depend upon individuals being aware of their rights and having the resources to exercise them. Those controls are inadequate substitutes for timely and effective Community-level enforcement, and the absence of such enforcement creates the danger of service-providers gravitating towards Member States with poor compliance records.[31]

The Partial Success of Self-help

> '[The Internet] requires a new paradigm for governance that recognizes the complexity of networks, builds constructive relationships among the various participants . . . and promotes incentives for the attainment of various public policy objectives in the private sector.' *Professor Joel Reidenberg.*[32]

In discussing Community activity, this book has necessarily focused on the failings of self-help rather than on its successes. Those failings have been shown to be substantial, as might be expected given the conditions of the online marketplace, in particular its capacity to support anonymity.[33] The 'trusted' third parties are sometimes less than neutral—the interests of payment intermediaries sometimes conflict with those of consumers; many privacy trustmarks are funded by industry and some have breached their promises on a number of occasions, as discussed in chapter 3 above.

[27] See Case 26/62, *Van Gend en Loos v Nederlandse Administratie der Belastingen* [1963] ECR I.

[28] See Case 14/83 *Von Colson and Kamann v Land Nordrhein-Westfalen* [1984] ECR 1891.

[29] See Cases C–C–6 & 9/90 *Francovich & Bonifaci v Italy* [1991] ECR I–5357.

[30] Case C–192/94, [1996] ECR I–1281.

[31] See generally, S Weatherill, 'Reflections on EC Law's 'Implementation Imbalance' in the light of the ruling in *Hedley Lomas*', in L Kramer and all (eds), *Law and Diffuse Interests in the European Legal Order* (Baden-Baden, Nomos Verlagsgessellschaft, 1997), who suggests that part of the solution may be to create Community-level enforcement agencies with powers to intervene at national level, at 52.

[32] 'Governing Networks and Rule-Making in Cyberspace', [1996] 45 *Emory Law Journal* 911 at 912.

[33] Ramsay has described the factors of marketplaces which favour the success of self-help as—low costs of compliance, small in-group conflict, a cohesive group, minimal third-party effects, low costs of detection of breach, effective sanctions, and credible threats: I Ramsay, *Consumer Protection* (London, Weidenfeld and Nicholson, 1989), at 91. It is clear that the electronic marketplace does not generally possess these characteristics.

The remedies offered by trusted third parties can also sometimes fail to protect consumers' interests. If a trader breaks a trustmark policy there is often little a consumer can do if his or her complaint is not dealt with properly. Software can be effective at protecting consumers from certain unwanted material and particular intrusions into their privacy, but is beyond the financial and technical means of many consumers. Authorship interests find little succour in pure self-help, whilst in relation to identity interests, the ICANN Uniform Dispute Resolution Process can be criticised from a European perspective as US-centric. The combination of a lack of effective remedies together with non-universality means that in general self-help leaves a good deal of room for Community activity.

Notwithstanding the failings of self-help, chapters 2 to 6 have highlighted some of its positive aspects. For consumers, the trusted third party can play an important role in bridging the gap to distant sellers. Many third parties have a global presence and do not suffer from the inertia of public regulators.[34] Credit card companies can guarantee the integrity of traders who would otherwise be entirely unknown quantities. Privacy seals can indicate to consumers that a Web-site acknowledges their concerns about personal data. Content-filtering software provides reasonably effective protection to those who can afford it and have the technical expertise to install it. Third parties can move quickly—a justifiable complaint about an offensive Web-site to a private filtering agent will generally result in immediate action and a large number of complaints to a credit card company about one particular merchant is likely to result in the rapid withdrawal of that merchant's credit facilities.

As regards producers, self-help has also been successful in the area of identity interests, the (albeit hybrid)[35] ICANN Process resolves most of the disputes brought to it within two months, an extraordinary timescale when compared to most court processes.

Community Dominance over the Member States?

The scale and content of the law discussed in this book indicate that it is the Community, rather than the individual Member States, which will dominate law-making in Europe's electronic marketplace.[36] Many of the instruments

[34] These advantages of self-help can also be seen to operate in the field of international commercial law, see generally C Chinkin, 'The Challenge of Soft-law: Development and Change in International Law' (1989) 38 *International & Comparative Law Quarterly* 850.

[35] It is noted here as in chapter 6 above that the ICANN Process is part-public and part-private.

[36] On the general theme of the Community's seemingly ever-increasing competence, see G de Burca, 'Reappraising Subsidiarity's Significance after Amsterdam', Jean Monnet Working Paper 7/1999, www.jeanmonnetprogram.org/; R Dehousse, 'Community Competence: Are there Limits to Growth?', in R Dehousse (ed), *Europe after Maastricht* (Munich, Law Books, 1994).

dealt with in this book are full or part measures of maximum harmonisation, including the Trade Mark Regulation, the Directive on privacy, the Directive on e-commerce and the Directive on the distance marketing of financial services.[37] The latter is the first Directive in the field of consumer transactions to aim at (part) maximum harmonisation.[38]

The instruments themselves encroach on areas which were previously the exclusive domain of the Member States. The Directive on distance contracts was the first Directive to encroach upon national rules regulating the execution of contracts (setting the maximum period for the seller to perform its part of the contract at 30 days).[39] The Directive on e-commerce requires Member States to 'ensure that court actions available under national law concerning information society services' activities allow for the rapid adoption of measures, including interim measures, designed to terminate any alleged infringement and to prevent any further impairment of the interests involved.' (Articles 18(1)). Given the traditionally slow movement of the wheels of justice in many countries, this provision may have considerable impact and it contrasts with the long-standing Community principle of national procedural autonomy in determining remedies, a principle which dictates that whilst the Community is empowered to establish substantive rules, it is for Member States to determine the means of achieving compliance with those rules.[40]

This expanding competence of the Community may be part of wider changes driven by the novel conditions of the electronic marketplace. In the

[37] Of course Directives and Regulations are supreme over inconsistent national law: Case 6/64, *Costa v ENEL* [1964] ECR 585: 'The integration into the laws of each Member State of provisions which derive from the Community, and more generally the terms and the spirit of the Treaty, make it impossible for the States as a corollary, to accord precedence to a unilateral and subsequent measure over a legal system accepted by them on a basis of reciprocity', at 593–4. See generally, P-C Muller-Graff, 'EC Directives as a means of private law unification', and W van Gerven, 'The ECJ case-law as a means of unification of private law?', in A Hartkamp and all (eds), note 14 above.

[38] Recital 8: 'Whereas the adoption by the Member States of conflicting or different consumer protection measures rules . . . would impede the functioning of the internal market.' Compare for example Article 8 of Directive 93/13 on Unfair Terms in Consumer Contracts: 'Member States may adopt or retain the most stringent provisions compatible with the Treaty in the area covered by this Directive, to ensure a maximum degree of protection for the consumer.' Of course some consumer law Directives outside the field of transactions have aimed at maximum harmonisation, see eg Directive 85/373/EEC on product liability (although its maximal nature is disputed, see further G Howells and T Wilhelmsson, *EC Consumer Law* (Aldershot, Dartmouth, 1997) at 47).

[39] Article 7.

[40] See in particular: Article 249 EC—'A directive shall be binding, as to the result to be achieved . . . but shall leave to the national authorities the choice of form and methods'. See also Case 158/80, *Rewe-Handelsgesellschaft Nord mbH v Hauptzollamt Kiel* [1981] ECR 1805, in which the European Court of Justice stated that, 'the Treaty . . . was not intended to create new remedies in the national courts', at 44.

field of censorship, it can be pointed out that the effectiveness of prohibiting material in one medium is undermined if the public can access it via the Web.[41] In chapter 3 it was described how US negotiations with the EU over the privacy rights of Europeans vis-à-vis US companies appear to have driven wider domestic discussion of that issue. Also, chapter 2 indicated how the Directive on e-commerce has driven a review of unfair competition law in Germany, which has been forced to consider whether its strict controls on advertising will place it at a disadvantage when the Directive's provisions on home country control come into force;[42] the Directive's liberalisation of advertising of professional services online has forced professional bodies in a number of countries to consider lifting their horizontal bans on advertising (rather than have the odd situation of professionals being able to promote themselves online but nowhere else).

Chapter 4 has shown how e-commerce may push the Community towards attempting to harmonise a part of Member States' criminal laws.[43] It can also be noted that the Council of Europe, often a path-breaker for the Community in the past,[44] has been active in the area, having adopted in 2001 its Cybercrime Convention.[45]

It would further seem that e-commerce is pushing the Community towards greater competence in the field of international agreements on jurisdiction and enforcement in civil and commercial matters. The Community adopted in 2000 the Brussels Regulation aiming at complete harmonisation of almost all of Member States' related rules in the context of the internal market and now that the Community has exercised this competence, it can be argued to have taken possession of the field so as to exclude the possibility of related Member State agreements with third countries. As the European Court of Justice held in the *ERTA* case:

> 'each time the Community, with a view to implementing a common policy envisaged by the Treaty, adopts provisions laying down common rules . . . the Member

[41] In April 2000 Channel 4 Television in the United Kingdom showed a version of a film—*A Clockwork Orange*—on the Web, which it was not permitted to show on television, in an effort to highlight what it saw as an arbitrary distinction:www.guardianunlimited.co.uk/freespeech/article/0,2763,21468,00.html (no longer available).

[42] It is noted again that the Directive on Comparative Advertising has also played a role here.

[43] This may include promised action on the current divergence of national laws in their treatment of electronic evidence, Commission, *A European Initiative in Electronic Commerce*, COM(97) 157 at III–4.

[44] For example in human rights (see Case 4/73, *Nold v Commission* [1974] ECR 491 and subsequent Treaty developments), and in data protection (see chapter 3 above).

[45] http://conventions.coe.int/. See also Council of Europe Recommendation R95/13 on the harmonisation of criminal procedural laws relating to information technology, 1995, covering issues such as search and seizure, technical surveillance, co-operation with investigating authorities, and cryptography: I Carr and K Williams, 'Council of Europe on the harmonisation of criminal procedural laws relating to information technology', [1998] *Journal of Business Law* 468.

> States no longer have the right, acting individually or even collectively, to undertake obligations with third countries.'[46]

Any Member State concluding an independent agreement in that field with a third country would risk distorting the internal market as the conditions for e-business would not be the same in that Member State as in others.

Autonomous or 'Americanised' Community Regulation?

There are many reflections of the United States within the phenomenon of e-commerce—consumerism, a predominance of the English language,[47] and an attachment to individual freedom—cultural strands which have been asserted by Latouche to be part of globalisation generally.[48] The Net was invented in the US, and in 2000 94 out of the 100 most-visited Web-sites were located there.[49] Many of the third parties discussed above in the context of self-help are based in the US—*VISA* in consumer protection, *TRUSTe* and *P3P* in privacy, *Safesurf* in the field of content filtering, and finally ICANN in the field of domain-identity.[50]

To what extent does Community regulation embody these reflections of the US? The evidence of this book points towards the broad *independence* of Community regulation. This can be seen particularly in the Community's insistence on jurisdiction over consumer contracts lying in the first instance with the courts of the consumer's country of domicile and on applying a public-law framework to privacy. On the other hand, there are parallels between Community and US regulation, for example in the field of ISP liability for copyright infringement.

[46] Case 22/70, *Commission v Council ('ERTA')* [1971] ECR 263 at para. 17.

[47] This may not be a lasting characteristic, at least it would seem likely that the most-used language on Web-sites may soon be Chinese.

[48] S Latouche, *The Westernization of the World* (Cambridge, Polity Press, 1996) at 3.

[49] Commission, *The organisation and management of the Internet: International and European Policy Issues 1998–2000*, COM(2000) 202, www.ispo.cec.be/eif/internetpoliciessite/organisation/com(2000)202.doc, at 33. It might further be pointed out that U.S litigiousness, combined with high levels of technological sophistication, mean that that country naturally has a good deal of influence in the development of relevant law as cases simply come up there first.

[50] It has been asserted that in global business regulation generally the United States carries more weight than the EU: P Braithwaite and G Drahos, *Global Business Regulation* (Cambridge University Press, 2000) at 475–8, (surveying 13 business sectors and finding the EU more influential than the US in only 3—prescription drugs, road transport and food standards).

The Global Aspect of the Community's Role

> '[There is a need for] a framework of international law, a universal body of law which mirrors the global character of the Internet.' *French President Jacques Chirac.*'[51]

Notwithstanding the argument that the Community has not gone far enough in protecting consumers' interests beyond its borders, the chapters above do indicate significant international activity on the part of the Community, activity which is paralleled on the part of private organisations representing consumers[52] and businesses.[53]

This Community activity includes:

Consumers' fair trading interests—The Community played an active role in negotiating the OECD's Guidelines on Consumer Protection, and in establishing the International Consumer Protection and Enforcement Network ('ICPEN').[54]

Consumers' privacy interests—The Directive on privacy broadly reflects the OECD's Guidelines on Transborder Data Flows, and the Community has concluded a series of agreements on privacy with third countries.

Consumers' morality interests—the Community contributed to the making of the Council of Europe's Cybercrime Convention and the Community has helped to establish a global network of hotlines concerning harmful content.

Producers' authorship interests—the Information Society Directive broadly reflects the World Intellectual Property Organisation's WCT and WPPT Treaties.

Producers' domain-identity interest—the Trade Mark Directive is consistent with the Paris Convention, the Trade Mark Regulation implements the TRIPS Agreement, and Regulation 733/2002 on '.eu' top level domain adopts WIPO's best practice policies on the use of trademarks in domain names.

[51] [Author's translation, from—'un état de droit international, un cadre juridique universel à la mésure du caractère mondial de l'Internet,']. Speech given at the G8 conference in Paris of May 2000, www.qlinks.net/items/qlitem7430.htm.

[52] Jim Murray, Director of the Bureau Europeén de Unions de Consommateurs ('BEUC'), has stated in a general context, 'BEUC's work is increasingly concentrated at a global level, as decisions taken there often have a great impact at regional and national levels', (quoted in D Harland, 'The Consumer in the Globalised Information Society: the Impact of the International Organisations', paper presented at the 7th International Consumer Law Conference, Helsinki, May 1999, 'The Consumer in the Globalised Information Society', at 26).

[53] See for example the International Chamber of Commerce's guidelines for marketing on the Net, *ICC Revised Guidelines on Advertising and Marketing on the Internet*, (www.iccwbo.org/commissions/marketing/internet_guidelines.html, 1998), and its E-Commerce Project dealing largely with business-to-business e-commerce: www.iccwbo.org/home/electronic_commerce/electronic_commerce_project.asp.

[54] www.icpen.org. ICPEN consists of twenty-nine member countries, including the EU member states, the United States, Canada, and Japan.

This activity feeds into a complex picture of international regulation of e-commerce, one which mirrors in many respects the nature of e-commerce itself—public and private, individual and collective, national and international. An effort is made below to describe this picture, and to compare it to a traditional regulatory model (the Community can be characterised as a 'State' for the purposes of these models).

Figure 1— Traditional model for regulating global activity:

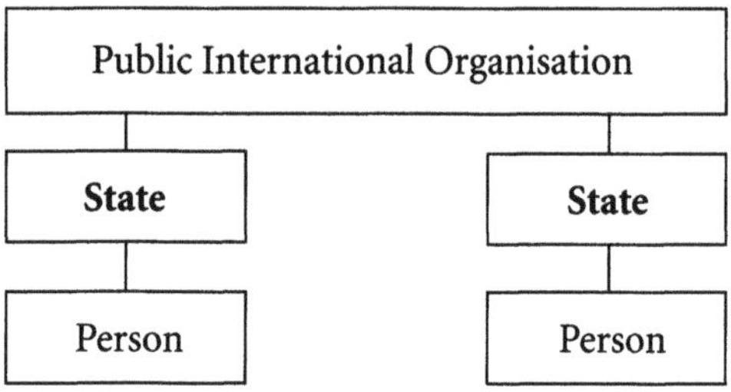

Figure 2— E-commerce inspired regulatory model:

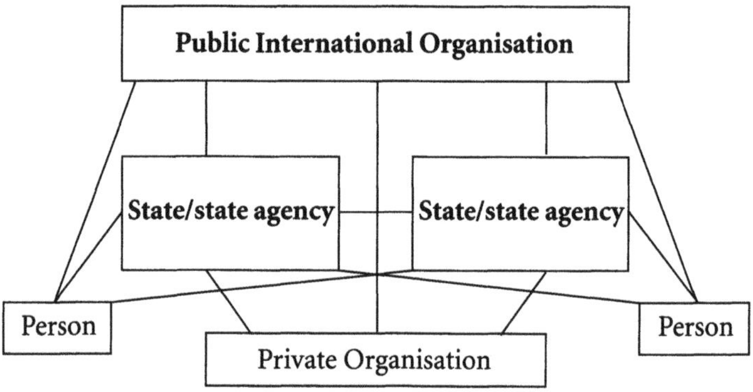

Figure 2 emphasises how external influences constrain the role of the State, which is itself fractionalised by the concentration of technical expertise in agencies, eg:

— within the Community, the role played by various Directorates-General of the Commission—Consumer Protection, Internal Market, and Telecommunications;[55]

[55] This 'fractionalisation' has been identified by Anne-Marie Slaughter as a feature of globalisation generally; she argues that State institutions now perform the functions of 'world government'—legislation, administration and adjudication: 'The Real New World Order' (1997) *Foreign Affairs* 183 at 184.

— within the US, the role of the FTC in regulating consumer protection, and the Department of Commerce in regulating privacy.

Figure 2 describes the increasing importance of public international organisations, such as WIPO, the Hague Conference and the OECD, an importance reflected in Community activity. Further, signs can be noted of public international bodies appreciating their relevance to those beyond the nation-state: WIPO consulted widely on the ICANN process,[56] the OECD admits accredited consumer bodies as observers, and the Hague Conference began in 1999 to keep the public up-to-date on its activities via its Web-site.[57]

Community regulation is further interlinked with *private* international organisations. Whilst international companies have long been closely concerned with the processes of international regulation, this book has indicated the important role in e-commerce regulation played by non-profit-making organisations such as ICANN, Consumers International, the World Wide Web Consortium, TRUSTe, and Privacy International.

E-commerce can be considered to be at an early stage of its development—the date it entered mainstream life in the Community might be fixed as late as 1999.[58] This book has shown that the Community is failing therein to protect the critical interests of consumers. There has been a political failure to bridge the divide between consumers' diffuse interests and the concentrated interests of producers. Perhaps the most important failure is the absence of manufacturer liability for goods not conforming to contract. Such liability is already a reality in a number of Member States and, within the Community, it would both provide consumers with an easily-accessible counter-party in their home country in respect of many goods bought abroad and better reflect the reality of modern consumer decision-making. The quicker that that failure and the others identified in this book are remedied, the quicker consumer e-commerce will reach its full potential.

[56] Chapter 6 above.

[57] www.hcch.net.

[58] This was the year Net-related stocks experienced their greatest surge, and when Web addresses became a regular feature of advertisements on television and in print (at least in the author's experience). The Net has come upon the world at a much greater speed than other mass media—in terms of time to reach 50 million users it took the telephone 74 years, the radio 38 years and the Web 4 years: per I Lloyd, *Electronic Commerce and the Law* (Edinburgh University Press, 2000) at 1.

INDEX

www.ingramcontent.com/pod-product-compliance
Ingram Content Group UK Ltd.
Pitfield, Milton Keynes, MK11 3LW, UK
UKHW021239300926
15471UKWH00013B/698